A British Family's attem|

CW01081295

1

Prologue – The Characters

Mike – The Author
Julie – His wife and the sensible one
Josh – Their Son – 12 at the start of this adventure
Lucy – Their daughter – 8 at the start of this adventure
Tia – The Old English Sheepdog

Mike

Mike was born in Hong Kong in 1961, his parents having fled England in the 1950's to achieve great success there in business. Educated at boarding school in England, he left to join the motor industry, and worked for Toyota, Ford and Volkswagen in The UK. He married Ann-Marie at the age of 18, and has two grown up children who live in Dorset. Ann-Marie died tragically of a brain tumour in the mid 90's. Mike then met "The absolute love of his life", Julie. The couple were married in October 2000, and the wedding was attended by Julie's two children, who now consider Mike "their Dad". Mike loves cars, motor racing, cooking and reading and has an extraordinary memory for trivia.

Julie

Julie was born and brought up in Warrington, Cheshire. Her parents instilled a work ethic into her from an early age and she joined a telecommunications company shortly after leaving school, and remained with them until leaving England at the start of this book. She married Robert after the birth of their two children Josh and Lucy. The marriage didn't work out as the couple had such different interests, and Julie met Mike on a corporate hospitality trip in Berlin. She shares Mike's passion for motor racing, cars and reading. She is a quietly assertive woman, who tackles physical tasks with an alacrity that belies her femininity.

Josh

Josh is an electrical genius, with an amazing understanding for circuits and current. He is certain that anyone below the age of 21 is both a music luddite and completely incapable of operating any piece of apparatus containing a silicon chip. His main

2

passion is music, which must always be played at high volume and with the bass turned up to maximum. His current favourite pastime is igniting his sister's very short fuse at every opportunity.

Lucy

Lucy is extremely competitive in all things. She follows her mother in being a natural all round athlete, and excels academically. She is a child who is capable of entertaining herself for hours on end, but is equally happy with a bunch of friends. A seemingly perfect daughter, the downside is a temper that would make the devil himself quake. When over-tired the rest of the household have been known to take refuge in other parts of the house.

Tia

Tia is an Old English Sheepdog, and is a simple soul. She is possibly the most stupid dog in the world, but that is her charm. She will cordially greet any strangers (including potential burglars) with head bowed and tail wagging. Now middle aged, she still behaves like a puppy, barking madly whenever she sees a chance to play, and sulking when the kids go off without her.

Chapter One - The Holiday

I approached the holiday with some trepidation. Although I desperately needed a break, the thought of two weeks in Lanzarote, in a two bedroom bungalow, with the mother-in-law, the sister-in-law and the two year old nephew joining our family didn't bode well for full-on rest and relaxation. Don't get me wrong, I'm blessed with the world's greatest mum in law, I dearly love my nephew, and his mum is fantastic too, but it did have the makings of a problem or two. Couple all of that with the fact that I had heard all about "Lanzagrotty" from many people over the years and you can probably share my concerns. However, having cut our cloth by having a hugely expensive wedding, finances dictated that this was all we could afford.

Things didn't start too well either. We arrived in the middle of the night – my first recollections are of a huge cactus garden at the airport and a very hot wind, exacerbated by the taxi driver's insistence that all his windows should be open, and the air conditioning resolutely in the off position. I have since learned that this is standard practice here, despite the fact that the cabs are all high specification Mercedes with fabulous climate control systems. It would seem that the drivers are convinced that the compressor will ruin their fuel consumption, and nobody has considered the fact that opening the windows on a modern car totally destroys the slippery, wind-tunnel perfected shape, to the extent that fuel is used even more dramatically than in "clean", air-conditioned trim.

We duly arrived at the villa at around one in the morning, hot, sweaty and tired. Whilst the house was beautiful, fully equipped and clean, we were alarmed to discover that there was no drinking water, absolutely no food, and not a loo roll in sight! I went to bed with a heavy heart, a dry mouth, and without my usual nightly bathroom visit.

All seemed well the next morning, however, when we woke to glorious sunshine and a spectacular view of the mountains. A short walk took us to the nearest supermercado where we stocked up on essentials, marvelling at the prices of booze and cigarettes. One of the many amazing things about Lanzarote is the quality

4

of the light. Unsullied by man-made pollution, one can see huge distances and everything looks so bright and clear. I was entranced by this as I looked at the sea that first day, and it still stops my heart to this day when I gaze at Fuerteventura off the Puerto Del Carmen coast.

My fears about the holiday turned out to be totally unfounded. We all spent the first week totally relaxing, getting tanned by day and playing slightly drunken cards each night. We hired a car and the magic of Lanzarote took a real hold on me. The very barrenness has an ethereal beauty, the low rise architecture standing stark, white and clean against the dark landscape. Lanzarote was first annexed by Spain in the 15th century, along with the six other Islas Canarias. The island struggled for many years due to its total lack of any natural water. Fishing and the farming of cochineal beetles for use as a red food colouring provided the only industry, the beetles thriving on the prickly pear cactus plants. Today, cochineal has been replaced by synthetic colorants, but the legacy is many acres of prickly pears along the north coast of the island.

As I began to feel the benefit of good weather and relaxation, I started to look at the people who were living on this Atlantic rock. They all seemed to be happy, and more than a little carefree. Nobody wore designer clothes, they didn't have expensive cars and they didn't ever appear to be hurrying. I superimposed an image of Julie and me rushing around in our expensive suits, tearing along the M6 in our flashy cars, and grabbing a few minutes with the children when we could. It was obvious who had the richer lives, although I had spent my entire career thinking otherwise.

I am a daydreamer. That's not to say I'm dim, but I do use up idle time enjoying the benefit of a very active imagination, and I began to daydream of living in Lanzarote. I imagined all the logistics of moving, I decided where we would live and what sort of transport we would have. I knew it was a dream with no base in reality, and I also knew that Julie would soon dispel the thought with a dose of her superb logic, so I didn't say anything until half way through the break. I'm pretty sure we were by the pool at the time, and I said something like "I could really live here." I waited for the logic bolt, and was amazed when she calmly responded "Me, too, what we need is a business idea,

5

maybe we could provide some kind of service for people like us visiting Lanzarote. Something that will help them to have a better holiday." I was totally stunned, she had obviously been thinking along the same lines as I had. But instead of dreaming about cars, motorcycles and palatial villas, she had, ever the pragmatist, been thinking about how we would earn a living.

We spent the remaining week of our holiday lounging around the pool, snorkelling at the beach and visiting the usual tourist haunts. All the while, however, we were plotting; both testing our ideas and carrying out as much research as we could, to provide ourselves with good data for when we returned to England. We did this clandestinely, because we didn't want to have to justify an idea that was still not even half-baked. All our thoughts and plans were written in a little note book we had purchased for 100 Pesetas, and which we cherish to this day. We found that we had already started looking at Lanzarote through different eyes, as a potential home for our family. At first I wondered if we were just providing ourselves with an interesting mental diversion while we relaxed, but as the week wore on, I really began to believe it would be possible.

I should tell you at this point about our business idea. The way Julie and I work is almost organic, and we had worked on many projects together for both our companies. We start with the germ of an idea, and flesh it out, and add to it over time. Because of our complimentary skills, we seem to be able to cover any plan from every angle - her skill is in finance and operations, mine in sales and marketing. My style is effusive, grand and enthusiastic. Julie injects caution and reality, posing difficult questions and filling in all the detail. But we work seamlessly, both contributing the big ideas, and both working them, either to death or living, breathing life. Our business idea was related to our own holiday experience and was simply this: Having been through the trauma of arriving at an empty house, having spent ages agonising over where to go, what to do and who we should use for car hire, a decent meal or any of the plethora of goods or services we might want to buy, we wanted to start a company offering just this kind of advice to fellow Britons visiting the island. It started as basically as that, and then evolved over the ensuing weeks to provide visitors with a whole range of benefits for a single payment prior to their holiday. They would have a welcome pack containing all the essentials placed in their villa

6

prior to arrival. We would visit them on their first day, and offer them advice on where to go and what to do during their stay, based on what they wanted from their holiday. We would give them a discount card providing them with best prices and guaranteed quality on a huge range of goods and services. They would have 24 / 7 access to a hotline to provide general advice or assistance in any emergency. And finally, we would hire them a whole host of essentials ranging from children's toy packs to camp beds and pushchairs, at low prices and without a deposit. What we had done, was to take everything that had caused us a problem on the holiday and address it by making it a part of our service. All we needed was a name, and once again Julie came good. She initially came up with the phrase "Fait Accomplis" or "Job Done", which summed up what we were offering beautifully. The only problem was that it was French. So she set about finding a Spanish equivalent, using a dictionary. She had a eureka moment after about ten minutes search -"Estupendo!" which means "Fantastic!" "Brilliant!" or "Job done!" Our business was born and had been christened.

I remember the last night of our holiday well. We all looked fabulous, with our deep tans and shiny eyes from days of complete relaxation. We walked along the seafront, stopping to take photos and admire another stunning Atlantic sunset. I didn't have the usual end of holiday blues - I knew by then that we would be coming back. I think Julie sensed a possibility, but she didn't share my conviction by that stage. I can remember saying to her that we shouldn't say good bye to the island, merely au revoir. My last words as the aircraft wheels left the tarmac were a whispered "We'll be back".

Chapter Two – The Planning

Arriving back to a cold and wet Manchester was a real shock. But our hearts were warmed by the prospect of the challenge that lay ahead. We needed to give our basic idea wings - we began to put together our plans and processes, to see if we could make it work, and we needed to look at our finances and devise a business plan to see if we could really afford to do it. At this stage we didn't talk to anybody. Even Josh and Lucy, though aware we were working on something, didn't know how serious we were. We wanted to have all the answers, and have all the bases covered before we started telling people what we were planning. We must have put in at least a hundred hours of our own time during that first week back. The basic idea took shape, we quickly worked out we could afford it if we sold the house, and we understood how our selling process would work. We must have visited a hundred or more websites, and quickly learned about the Spanish economy and fiscal systems, and studied reams of statistics on Canary island visitors. We got information from The British High Commission and spoke to both the English schools on the island. We started talking to a freight company who would ship our belongings over there, and we even began the design of the Estupendo website. We also wrote to George and Joy Paterson, who own the villa in which we had been staying during our holiday. They spend their winters in Lanzarote and their summers near Bedford in the United Kingdom. We gave them a brief insight into our plans and invited them to let us know if they could offer any advice.

Julie and I have always had a theory about anything that we have tackled in life. Our theory is "If it's meant to work out, it will", and we've always found that somehow things just fall into place for us when we need them to. The very fact that we were together was as a result of this logic. And so it was with our planned move. Our first break was that Joy responded to our letter with a telephone call, to tell us that a friend owned a villa less than 100 metres from hers, and that his long term tenants were leaving. We subsequently got in touch with the owner and he agreed to a two-year tenancy. We'd be based in the heart of Puerto del Carmen and would be using the same communal pool we had enjoyed so much during our holiday.

8

So began the next phase of our plan - extricating ourselves from the UK. The first task was to put the house on the market. We approached three local agents and one stood out as being more professional. Brooklands were duly awarded the franchise to sell our house - their managing director had promised to have viewers within a week and an offer by the end of September - this seemed quite remarkably to fit in with the ambitious time-scale we had set ourselves. Our part of the bargain was to get the house fit for sale, which was no mean feat! Nine years of young growing children and an assortment of pets had inflicted more than fair wear and tear on our semi in Stockton Heath. But having watched numerous make over programs on cable TV we were more than up to the task, and didn't use any MDF! Surprisingly everything came together and we ended up in the daft situation where our house looked better than it ever had before, and all we wanted to do was move on. True to their word, Brooklands sent a steady stream of viewers to the house and within 3 weeks a charming couple made an offer and the legal wheels were set in motion. I cannot speak highly enough of the estate agent, and the manner in which they conducted the whole transaction. The solicitors however, were another story......

I should tell you that the solicitors for both parties had offices in Stockton Heath almost directly opposite each other. Door to door I would estimate to be less than 40 metres. I mention this because they insisted on every document travelling by Royal Mail between both their premises and our homes, which resulted in some incredibly frustrating delays in the completion process. I'll give you one example: Their solicitor sent a letter to ours one Friday asking 3 simple questions. This letter duly arrived with our solicitor on the Monday, and sat somewhere in his office until the Thursday when he forwarded the letter to us, again asking the same 3 questions. This arrived with us on the Friday; fortunately I was able to collect the mail, as I wasn't at work that day. I immediately phoned the solicitor and answered the 3 questions. Result - one full week lost.

We quickly realised what was happening, as did the couple who had elected to buy our house, and wherever possible we by-passed the legal system, both updating and conferring with each other at every stage. I am sure this caused the solicitors much

9

consternation but the result was that despite their ineptitude we were able to complete only a couple of weeks behind schedule.

During this time we had to give notice at work. At both Julie's and my company redundancies were in the air – businesses were feeling the pinch of a mini recession. This put us in a difficult position, as we didn't want people to lose their jobs when we knew we were leaving anyway. Because of this we both spoke to our employers earlier than planned. For me the result was amazing, as I was put on garden leave and was able to continue planning for our future, whilst being paid and still enjoying the benefit of my company car. For Julie it was a little trickier, as she had a long and detailed handover process to go through, and preferred to wait until contracts had been exchanged before risking resigning from a 14-year career. To my frustration, she had to work until the week before we were due to leave. This left me in the unaccustomed role of House Husband and school delivery driver, as well as chief planner and box packer.

The total time from offer to completion on the house was 7 weeks and during this time we had been busy sorting our entire life's possessions into 4 categories. The first was all the things we wanted to go by sea - this was relatively easy as we set up a simple boxing factory in our back room. The second category was also simple - all the things we wanted to throw away, and I would estimate we made 60 trips to the recycling plant. The third category was the relatively small number of items we planned to take with us by air - the nightmare being our rather large computer. The final category was all the good stuff we had no need for that we decided to sell. We therefore made a list, priced everything up and distributed details to friends and family. I was delighted when a colleague of mine ticked off a number of items on the list and promised she would be round with a van the following weekend. At this point we were still some 3 weeks away from moving out of our home and still 6 weeks away from Lanzarote. I waved them off in the van clutching a fat roll of money, with a self- satisfied smile on my lips. My delight was short lived when Julie pointed out to me that I had sold, among many other things, our toaster, our kettle and our microwave! I have to say I wasn't particularly popular until I remedied the situation a week or so later by borrowing the items from my Father-in-law, Bill's, empty house. Needless to say that

10

whenever a brew was needed during that week, it was my job to put the saucepan on!

We had arranged to stay in Bill's house for the short time between moving out of our home and travelling to Lanzarote, and I spent the week leading up to our move in a state of nervous anticipation. I need to tell you some things about my family at this point. Julie and the kids are the lights of my life, but they do have a few, tiny weaknesses. The two most common traits they all share are a complete inability to meet deadlines and a generally poor approach to any kind of team working. I should say that I am convinced this only applies to their home lives and not at work or school, never the less you will understand why I approached a house move, which requires both of the above skills in abundance, with trepidation. I have to say that my fears were totally unfounded. With the exception of Lucy, who was after all only 8, we all worked like Trojans, and the task was accomplished without any mishaps. This was despite many friends taking advantage of the fact that we had a van at our disposal, and this entailed several unscheduled trips around Warrington. I have already mentioned my many trips to the local tip and the staff there had become accustomed to me arriving in either one of our cars laden with "useful" stuff. Imagine their faces when I arrived with a whole van full on our departure day!

We actually moved out of the house a week before completion, to give ourselves the opportunity to clean it. In the event, because of the problems surrounding Julie's departure from work I ended up doing this job over 3 days on my own, with a stinking cold. It gave me an opportunity to reflect on how the mighty can fall, having swapped my designer suit and posh office for a bottle of bleach and a pair of marigolds. Seeking sympathy from my beloved, I was met with a terse "Any woman would have done the job in one day!" Had the tone for our future working relationship been set?
If times ever get tough in Lanzarote, contract cleaning will be an option!

And so we moved into Julie's Dad's home. A nice little place, but not designed for 4 humans, 1 dog and 10 cubic metres of shipping freight! Those final two weeks certainly tested our ability to deal with stress, and the prospect of our longest ever holiday was the only thing that kept us sane. In a bid to keep

11

everyone going I resorted to posting a daily notice on the fridge showing the number of days of work and school left to departure. Just to add flavour to this recipe the weather duly turned cold and damp in true northern English style. One light in this firmament was the fact that our bank balance seemed to have an enormous number of digits, having sold the house. We were therefore able to embark on a mini-spending spree, consoling ourselves with some serious retail therapy. This also meant that we were able to confirm the flights, book our car hire, and arrange our various good-bye flings. Our bank caused us much amusement. For the previous two years they had responded to overdraft requests with some reluctance, and certainly hadn't bent over backwards to assist us when times were tough. Within a week of our house sale money being deposited, however, we received a letter from them telling us we had "been specially selected to receive a platinum credit card" I took great delight in filing the letter in the bin. Pounds were no good to us now that we were Peseta multi-millionaires!

So far I've talked about Julie, Josh, Lucy and myself. I should mention that we were a family of six, the other two members being of the canine and feline persuasion. Smokey the cat was by now 13 years old, and became a member of my family as a kitten. She started life in Dorset, moved with me to Derby and finally settled in Warrington when I met Julie. She has never been a particularly social animal, and chose to live al fresco in a little house in our front garden in Stockton Heath. Given her age and lack of sociability we felt it would be imprudent to subject Lanzarote to Smokey! We therefore decided to "retire" her back to her roots in Dorset, and we settled her in with my Daughter Natalie, where she enjoyed life in a cottage with many open fields. Tia is an Old English Sheepdog, who had been part of Julie's family for 4 years. At no point did we consider leaving Tia behind. I could write a book on Tia's antics, and probably will. Suffice to say she is completely mad and totally adorable. Since the advent of passports for pets we had thought that it would be relatively easy to transport her to Lanzarote. The reality was 3 visits to the vet, an awful lot of paperwork, a huge cost and a fair amount of stress. At the end of the day it cost considerably more to get Tia to Lanzarote than the rest of the family put together. As an aside, Lanzarote customs at that time closed at one o'clock each day (how quaint is that?). We therefore had to arrange to fly the day before her in order to clear her through customs prior to her arrival.

We had no intention of remaining "extranjeros" (foreigners) when in Spain, and we decided early on that we would learn the language. We bought a computer-based program and some excellent compact discs produced by a man called Michel Thomas. I heartily recommend this man for language learning, if you are able to ignore the clicking and sucking of his false teeth, and the abysmal toupee he so obviously wears in the grinning picture on the cover of the cd's!

The reaction of our friends was universal with only one exception. They all expressed envy and a suppressed desire "to do the same, one day." The exception was Stuart the mobile phone man, who I had called to remove the telephone kit from my car. "Why would you want to start a business in Lanzarote, and not here?", he asked. I looked up at the dark sky, zipped my jacket up against the bitter North wind and pulled my cap on to keep the rain off. I looked Stuart straight in the eye and said "I have absolutely no idea, mate" It won't surprise you to know that my brilliant ironic timing was totally lost on Stuart who remains amazed that we would ever have wanted to leave Warrington and the UK economy behind.

Our final week in the UK was all about saying goodbye to our many friends and family. It was a super week which we started with a pamper session at Carden Park (a beautiful hotel in Chester) and included numerous lunches and many brief visits. One of the highlights was on the final Thursday, when Julie went shopping with her Mum, who bought her some stunning earrings which will always remind us of our last few days in Warrington. Her fiancé Norman and I then met up with the girls and we had a memorable lunch in Stockton Heath's newest, poshest restaurant. The strange thing is that each time we met with people to say goodbye, they would ask us "when are you coming to say goodbye?" Inevitably this left us with a feeling of running around in ever decreasing circles. In order to avoid this problem becoming too big, we arranged for all our colleagues, friends and family to join us for a final night out. I was delighted that so many people were able to come and we boogied the night away and finished up in a curry restaurant with our two closest friends Chris and Sharon. They finally dropped us at home at around 3

13

o'clock, and Chris and I embraced in a manly and slightly drunken hug, both clearing our throats heartily!

We had agreed that the following day would be Christmas day. True to form, I awoke with a hangover and Julie awoke with a stinking cold - so it really did feel like Christmas. By tradition Jenny, Julie's Mum, always conjures up a terrific Christmas dinner with a little bit of help from the rest of us. As always the meal was excellent and it was fun exchanging gifts and small talk with the family prior to our departure. This was a full on Christmas dinner, with decorations, gifts and too much sherry for grandma.....and it all took place on the 1st of December, much to the bemusement of Jenny's neighbours.

There was a poignant moment after we left Jenny's, as we had to drop Julie's company car and mobile phone at her office. This was our very last tie to corporate life - we really were on our own now.

As soon as we got home from the Christmas meal it was time to pack the final cases. For some time I had suspected that we would exceed our luggage allowance - we were after all bringing enough clothes to last us two months, a decent supply of kid's toys and our desktop PC. I had purchased a pair of bathroom scales in order to predict the potential damage at check in. When we weighed the cases we were both horrified to discover that we were some 60 kilos over - or around £350 in excess charges! But by this time it was close to midnight and we were due to get up in less than 5 hours, so we decided to leave the cases as they were and to take our chances at the airport.

Jenny and Norman kindly picked us up at 5 o'clock exactly. I will always remember the journey - 4 adults, 2 children, 1 dog and 148 kilos packed into an elderly Granada Estate. I don't think there was a spare bit of space anywhere in the car! We dropped Tia off with Julie's sister Sally who had kindly agreed to deliver her to the airport the following day for her own flight. Jenny and Norman joined us in the checkout queue, and as we got closer to the desk the sweat broke out on my forehead as I contemplated the fact that we seemed to have 3 times more luggage than anybody else. At these moments of crisis many thoughts go through your mind and I began to wonder if they would even let us on the plane. As I handed tickets and

14

passports to the girl on the counter I delivered what will always remain the greatest under statement in history "*some* of our bags may be a *little* overweight" In the event she didn't bat an eyelid or charge us a penny. It was hard to say our final good-byes at the departure gate, but we knew that we would see Jenny and Norman very soon.

The aircraft departed Manchester exactly on schedule, having been de-iced, and I looked down at a crisp bright Cheshire dawn, wondering when I would see England again. The weather throughout the flight was remarkably cloud free and Julie and I drank champagne as we watched Europe unfold beneath us. We had been particular about booking seats on the port side of the aircraft in order to get the best view of the approach to Arrecife. We were able to pick out many landmarks including "our" beach as the aircraft slowly descended to the airfield. As the wheels touched I muttered quietly "I said I'd be back." It was less than 4 months since the start of the fateful holiday that had changed our lives.

Chapter Three – The Arrival

We managed to get through customs without being lifted, and after a short search we found the car hire representative who took me to the short term car park to hand over my pre-booked Seat Cordoba. He apologised profusely as the car had automatic transmission, which didn't worry me at all. Not one word was said about the condition of the car, which I can only describe as the saddest, sorriest, specimen I have ever seen. The paint would once have been metallic silver, but it looked more like primer grey. Every single panel on the car had at least one dent or scrape. The slightest imperfection in the road surface caused a cacophony of squeaks and rattles, and the wheel bearings hummed loudly like a swarm of bees. The only good thing about the car was that the engine and transmission were in perfect order. The whole thing reminded us of a sad little donkey with a willing heart but a failing body. The Seat quickly became known in the family as "Burro". Burro was subsequently retired from the car hire fleet and now lives a quiet life in Puerto Del Carmen, and we often pass the car with the whole family shouting "Hola Burro!"

Inevitably the cases wouldn't fit in the car, so the girls were dispatched in a taxi and the boys followed in Burro. I surprised myself by driving straight to the villa with no wrong turns and I was finally able to see the place I had imagined so vividly for so many months. The bungalow was in a charming community called Las Villas, it had an enormous patio, some of which was shaded, and the gardens include cacti and a gigantic double trunked palm tree. One can start on a lounger at one end of the patio at dawn and follow the sun to its final rays at the other end.

Our first day in Lanzarote consisted of quickly unpacking, visiting the supermarket to buy essentials and introducing ourselves to Joy and George, without whom we wouldn't have secured our new home. We also began our acclimatisation, having jumped straight from sub zero Manchester to balmy 30 degrees Lanzarote.

Our second day's primary task was to land Tia safely and get her home. We headed for the Island's capital Arrecife to find the offices of our appointed customs agent, and ended up pounding

16

the streets of the city in search of a one-room first floor office in what seemed like unbearable heat. When we eventually located the company we were introduced to our contact Juan. He took copies of our documents but then told us that we were missing the essential airway bill, without which it "would not be possible" - he told us that we would need this document faxed to him within 45 minutes. We retired to the nearest bar and finally got through to the freight company in Manchester who faxed the bill through in the nick of time. Juan then asked us to return at 4 o'clock, which we did, only to be told it "would not be possible" as the aircraft had not landed. We explained to him that the aircraft was not due until 7.30pm, and after much debate with his boss he agreed that we should return at that time.

I was by now convinced that this would go horribly wrong as Juan didn't seem capable of carrying out the rather complicated task of clearing a live animal through customs, I also knew that Arrecife customs closed at lunchtime and that he should have carried out the clearance in the morning. I drove home with a heavy heart. I had not shared my fears with the family, but I had previously read a story about a dog which had arrived at its destination frozen stiff and very dead as the pilot had forgotten to turn on the cargo heating. By now I had convinced myself that in the unlikely event that Tia would actually arrive alive, she would be spending god knows how long at the mercy of Arrecife customs.

Dinner was eaten with much nervous laughter and Julie and I set off once again for Arrecife. This time Juan greeted us with a smile and the words "it is possible". He delivered the customs clearance form and his very reasonable bill with a flourish and gave us directions to the airport cargo centre, telling us it would be quite alright to go down the road marked no entry! As we walked through the door an armed guard greeted us with the word "Perro?" (Dog?) and proceeded to examine our paperwork and produce yet another form. He then gave me the form and pointed me in the direction of a very serious looking woman who again examined the two forms and added a third. She finally gestured for us to go in to the warehouse where Julie quickly spotted an enormous box containing our beloved sheep dog. Julie quickly led her outside, as by this time it had been over 8 hours since she had last had a wee. As she disappeared through the door another armed officer shouted "Señor!" At this point,

17

having invested so much time and perspiration in getting the dog here I seriously considered shouting to Julie "Run for it!" Fortunately discretion became the better part of valour and I turned to the guard who simply wanted to take all my paperwork from me. Tia seemed to have no ill effects from her ordeal, and as I headed Burro away from the airport I had an enormous lump in my throat as I reflected on the fact that all five of us were now safely in Lanzarote – we had made it!

Chapter Four – Telefonica and Maximo

Everybody who lives in Spain seems to have a story to tell about Telefonica, the national telephone company, and we had heard a few prior to our arrival. A telephone line was essential to our business and would get us back in contact with the virtual world via our website, so I set off one morning to call the company from the nearest payphone. Julie was amazed when I came back less than 10 minutes later saying "All sorted, the phone's being installed in three day's time!"

We woke up on the appointed morning full of excitement, as we were all looking forward to sending and receiving e-mails from all our friends. Inevitably, nobody showed up and I called the helpline. Unlike my first call, this one was to follow a pattern with which I was to become all too familiar. It's disconcerting to be put on hold (with the inevitable electronic music) before you've even spoken to anyone, and even worse to have to wait up to 20 minutes before doing so. Once through to the first person, one needs to ask to be put through to the English department, and this usually results in a further 20 minute wait. On this first occasion I was asked for all my details and then calmly assured that I hadn't ordered a new line. I explained that I had spoken to them three days previously and that an engineer had been due to call that very day. I was asked if I wanted to make a complaint, and replied that I simply wanted a telephone line. So a new order was taken, with installation promised five days further on.

This exact scenario occurred three further times during the next two weeks. Each time I resisted the offer of making a complaint and pleaded that I just wanted the line. And then one afternoon we suddenly broke out of this cycle of doom, when an unmarked white van pulled up outside the house and a short man with a huge moustache introduced himself as Maximo from Telefonica. I resisted the urge to embrace him, and took him straight inside. Once in the house he asked me where the "Buzon de telefono" was situated. Realising he meant the box, I pointed to the cream coloured box on the wall, which was clearly marked "Telefonica." "No, no!" He said and then spoke a fast stream of Spanish which was beyond me. Asking him to repeat himself, he simply did so, but faster and louder! Realising that I didn't understand him, he beckoned for me to follow him and we

19

walked all around the house looking for the buzon on the outside walls. He stopped at both the water and electricity boxes and tutted, and then he stood with his hands on his hips looking perplexed. I was worried now that he might give up, so I enlisted the help of some neighbours, thinking they would know what we were looking for. They all agreed that the buzon was the box I had originally pointed to inside the house, but Maximo shook his head firmly and went looking along the street. He could be seen for the next hour or so, peering into manhole covers, opening boxes in other people's walls and staring at the mass of wires in the nearest automatic exchange, all the while muttering and scratching his head. Eventually he wandered back to the house took the cover off the box on our wall, put a tester on it and proudly pointed to it exclaiming "Buzon!!" I shared his joy, and chickened out of pointing out that at least 5 people had told him that this was indeed the telephone buzon over the preceding hour or so. Maximo spent a few minutes fiddling inside the box, then explained that he had to go the main exchange and do some work there, but that he would be back shortly. As he drove away, I wondered if he would indeed return as it was now after 6 in the evening.

Dinner came and went, and I was on the point of screwing the cover back onto the box when Maximo returned triumphantly. He then produced another box and drilled the wall to fit it. He seemed to drill the holes completely randomly, so that the second box was a long way from lining up with the first and miles away from being level. Once again he disappeared for an hour or so, and then returned asking if I would like my new telephone to be blue, black or white. There then followed a fairly lengthy discussion involving the whole family, with Maximo first extolling the virtues of the white phone, and suddenly switching to the benefits of black, and avoiding dirty finger marks. We all finally agreed on black and he went back out to the van, only to return saying "I've only got blue, so that will have to do."

Maximo finally departed at around 10 o'clock, leaving us finally in touch with the outside world, and with a very wonky buzon. Little did we know that he would come back into our lives almost a year later!

Chapter Five – Woo and Speedy Gonzales

Prior to our arrival, we had enrolled the kids into the local English private school, and had booked a visit for us all to meet the headmaster, Roger Deign. As the Christmas holidays were approaching, we expected them to start in the new term, but Roger suggested that they should start immediately, as it would give them a chance to make friends locally. Neither Josh nor Lucy were particularly impressed with this, but they were duly sent the following day to their new school. Colegio Hispano Britanico is a terrific institution, originally started by Roger when he arrived on the island, to ensure that his own kids received a decent education. The school has a wonderful, informal style, with no uniforms, and everyone, teachers included, using only first names. However, everyone works hard and the results are impressive, with many kids going on to top international universities.

With the kids off our hands, we decided to use the time to sort our transport out. We had given ourselves a clear brief and budget. A small secondhand hatchback – the main stipulation being that it should have air conditioning, and a used scooter. We didn't have enough money to buy two cars, so the scooter would fulfil the need for separate means of travelling, whilst at the same time providing a practical and very economical way of getting about the island.

We rather naively thought that buying a car was as simple as walking into a showroom with a lot of money, and driving away a few days later. Not so in Spain, as we quickly found out. It is impossible to register a car in Spain without proving where you live. Unfortunately, the many documents we had proving our address were irrelevant, we need a form called a "Certificado de empadronamiento", which we had to obtain from our local Ayuntamiento, or town hall. The process is straightforward, but very long winded. You must first present yourself at the town hall, with passport and house deeds or rental contract. We did so, only to be told that our rent contract wasn't legal as it needed "stamping". The clerk explained that to make it legal we had to visit the stamp shop in the capital, Arrecife, and have it made official. Jumping into our hire car, Julie and I checked we had both understood the explanation in the same way, and set off for

Arrecife following the very explicit directions. The shop we were directed to was indeed a shop selling postage stamps. We gave the girl at the desk our contract and she seemed to know immediately what was required. She performed a very elaborate percentage calculation and told us how much we needed to pay. Mystified, we handed the money over and she then proceeded to affix postage stamps to that value all over the contract! This obviously did the trick because the clerk at the Ayuntamiento then accepted the contract and told us to return for our certificate three days hence. In the meantime we should expect a visit from an official at any time to check that we indeed were in residence. Nobody ever showed up, but we did collect our certificate on time and set off finally to buy a car.

I had expected the island to be flooded with ex-hire cars for sale cheaply, but in fact they all go back to the mainland to be sold off, so good used cars are hard to find on Lanzarote, and command ridiculous prices when compared to new ones. Some friends had recommended that we visit a dealer in Arrecife who we were told spoke quite good English. Having studied the map we arrived in Calle Portugal, a road that is now known in the family as Calle Poo-tugal, because it consistently smells like the worst sewage farm on the planet. I don't know what creates the smell, but it is there whatever the weather. I like to think that it is some kind of revenge being played on the inhabitants of the nearby Inalsa (water company) building, but who knows. Anyway, we boldly walked into the showroom and introduced ourselves to the owner, Luis, whose name we had been given. He looked totally blankly at us, and we mentioned our friends' name. Again a blank look. After much embarrassed shuffling, we realised that Luis had absolutely no English, so this would be an interesting transaction. Nevertheless, we persevered and explained in our best Spanglish that we needed a small hatchback with air conditioning. "Ah, Si!" Exclaimed Luis, and disappeared through the front door. We ambled around the cars on display, conscious that we had become responsible for his entire stock, and wondering when he would return. After about 20 minutes, there was a horn toot from outside and we wandered out to see Luis in a huge Daewoo saloon. He beckoned us in to join him and we set off on a test drive. The car was large, comfortable, well equipped and patently not a small hatchback, although it did have the distinction of being in perfect condition – a very rare thing in island cars more than a week old. Luis had seemingly

22

instantly realised how to sell to me, and proceeded to demonstrate the many electronic toys and the very powerful air-conditioner. Within a few kilometres I was sold, and just had to start work on Julie. Luis brilliantly played on her fear of the bureaucratic processes, explaining that he would take care of everything, and we could have the car within a few days. As good as his word, we picked the car up days later and purred away from the showroom. All that remained was for the family to name the car, and we duly christened it "Woo", a suitably oriental sounding name.

With the car sorted, we turned our attention to the scooter, and this proved even more difficult. We visited every scooter shop in town, and they all insisted that we needed our Resident's cards to buy any kind of motor vehicle. We knew this wasn't the case, as we had already purchased a car, so we headed back to Luis for advice. We explained our problem to him and he smoothly said that he would get us a second-hand scooter. He knew of a Malaguti "just inside our budget", and suggested we come back the next day to see it in his showroom.

As we walked in the next evening, I was surprised to see the most gorgeous, sexy Aprilia parked front and centre. Luis greeted us as old friends and showed us to the back of the showroom, where he had parked a very sad and sorry looking Malaguti. He enthusiastically pointed out the features of the bike, and even tried to start it, although it died after a fitful putter. I told him that I really wanted something a bit better, and I then witnessed a wonderful piece of acting. Luis looked towards to sparkling Aprilia and hesitated. He then looked dolefully at the floor and said he would try to find something for me. Like a lamb to the slaughter, I said "How much is the Aprilia?" "Oh, Senor Cliffe, it is brand new, the latest model, with fuel injection, muy, muy especial." Any sane man would have stopped at that point, but I ploughed on with "Well, how much is it?" Luis then took us to the machine, and with Josh slavering, talked us through the many features and all of their benefits, ensuring that we were positioned in such a way that we couldn't help seeing the forlorn Malaguti in the background. He finished his piece with "Look, forget this machine, let me find you something like the Malaguti, give me a few days or weeks." Of course, it was really all over by then anyway, we agreed a price

23

and collected the bike as our late Christmas present, and inevitably the Aprilia became known as Speedy Gonzales.

Woo did sterling service for us during our first six months or so, but the car simply wasn't suited to Lanzarote. It was too big to park easily, extremely susceptible to knocks and scrapes, and did not like off-road driving, which is a fact of life here. All of that, coupled with the fact that there was no hatchback for Tia meant he had to go, and he was eventually replaced by a Citroen hatchback which suited our needs far better.

Speedy remained with us for a few years, a cherished and hard-working part of the family. I was initially disappointed in the performance, as it was meant to be very fast despite being only 50cc's. I did some research on the internet, and discovered that the engine could be re-mapped using, of all things, a Gameboy console. I kept checking back on the website, fearing some kind of joke was being played on me, but it was there in black and white. So I set off for the local Aprilia dealer where I met Felix. I explained to him that I wanted my bike to be "Mas Rapida", and he fired a stream of Spanish back to me, which I didn't understand. At this point we both resorted to sign and sound language. It turned out that he was trying to establish whether I wanted quick acceleration, with a lower top speed, or vice versa. I explained that I wanted the latter, but the only way we could communicate was by making the sounds of a scooter accelerating quickly or slowly and then settling into either a low rev or high rev state. After a few minutes of this we had attracted a large crowd of kids from the street outside, who were in hysterics at the site of two grown men making motorcycle noises. We got there in the end and Felix duly reached into a large filing cabinet, and pulled out a bright green Gameboy. He flipped a cover off the bike's instrument panel, plugged in the little machine and keyed a series of codes. Job done, he took €15 from me and said goodbye. I sceptically fired the bike up and headed for the main road. Up until this point Speedy had always topped out at 70KMH, and I had developed the habit of going everywhere flat out. After Felix's efforts, Speedy finally lived up to his name, reaching 120KMH on the flat, and quite a bit more downhill. Amazingly, fuel consumption wasn't affected, and we consistently gave much bigger machines a fright in the usual Spanish traffic light drag races.

24

Chapter Six – Discovering Lanzarote

The first few months of our new lives were a wonderful period of discovery, and we all quickly realised that this little island was going to become our permanent home. We arrived in mid-winter, which roughly translates to the very best summer weather available in the UK. It was a joy to go out exploring in shorts and tee-shirts. We set out to become experts on the island and its history, and this has stood us in good stead with our business, as we can offer a genuine insight into every area of Lanzarote. I was staggered just recently to meet someone who has lived here for 20 years, but who has never ventured north of The Cactus Gardens, leaving a huge chunk (and arguably the most beautiful part of the island) unexplored.

It's easy to dismiss Lanzarote as a barren, volcanic rock. But there is a beauty and a drama in the landscape which never ceases to catch my breath. We made it our business to visit all the usual tourist places, so we did The Timanfaya trip, we hired quads to race up to Famara and Teguise, we visited Manrique's house, The Mirador del Rio and The Jameos del Agua. But we also parked the car and walked miles into the hills, visiting small villages and working fincas.

Our lifestyle and eating habits changed very quickly. Whilst it's possible to live here and enjoy pretty much everything you're used to in UK, we were determined to avoid using British shops, bars and restaurants. We have become devoted fans of the Tapas style of eating – small, tasty dishes of different foods, served at regular intervals and always accompanied by icy beer or good red wine. Our favourite tapas bars are in Arrieta and on the sea front in Playa Honda. For less than €10 per head, one can enjoy several hours of food, drink, sunshine and good conversation on a Sunday afternoon. Another early discovery was the traditional Spanish sociedad. I suppose the nearest equivalent would be the British Working Men's club. The licence to run the sociedad is passed from one family to another in a village every three years. Most villages have one, and most of them serve food. They all offer spectacular value for money. Our favourite is in Guatiza, and we visit it frequently. Our most recent meal there was with another couple, and we each had prawn starters, steak main courses and enjoyed four rounds of drinks – the bill was €45!

25

Sociedads can seem daunting at first, they are very noisy – most of the men seem to spend their time there playing cards and arguing – and the décor often leaves a little to be desired, but venture in, and the very fact that you are a foreigner brave enough to visit will ensure a very warm welcome. People will simply walk over to you and start talking, and they are without exception very kid friendly places.

The island is made up of seven municipalities, almost like counties in the UK. They are:

Arrecife

Arrecife covers an area of around 28 square kilometers and is home to around 40,000 people (more than a third of the island's population).

The port did not establish itself until the fifteenth century when the island began to trade with Spain and other nations. The harbour area was the best on Lanzarote, and Arrecife quickly became the gateway to Teguise, which was then the capital. Less salubrious inhabitants of Arrecife at this time included slave traders and pirates, preying on the busy shipping routes. This proved a problem for local inhabitants who left the island in droves until they were stopped by a Royal Decree preventing emigration!

A wooden fort was built to protect the port in the late 1500's, but it was burned down after only a few years, to be replaced by the present Castillo San Gabriel, which was designed by the Italian engineer Leonardo Torriani. His design included the now famous Puente de Las Bolas, or "Ball Bridge" which appears in so many photographs.

The year 1722 almost put paid to Arrecife for ever. The area was hit by a storm of such intensity that almost all the buildings were destroyed and many families left Lanzarote for good. Strangely, the massive eruptions of 1730 lead to Arrecife being re-established by people displaced from their homes in Yaiza.

In 1778 The Castillo San José was built to overlook the fishing harbour and to provide further protection from foreign ships. The island was famously attacked by some British privateers during

26

this period, and local inhabitants fought them bravely using camels. It seems that the British won the day, but soon left, realising that there was nothing of value to claim.

The early 1800's saw the church of San Ginés consecrated, and the population rose to about 5000, making it by far the largest town on the island, and leading it to be made the capital in 1852, with the construction of a new town hall. Trade consisted almost exclusively of fishing at this time, and the catch was salted on arrival at the port, and put out for display.

During the late nineteenth and early twentieth centuries Arrecife became the focal point of Lanzarote, with all the islanders visiting the capital to sell their produce, or to meet the twice weekly mail boats, or even to marvel at the new-fangled oil powered street lamps!

Arrecife evolved along at a steady pace through latter years, being indirectly affected by the tourism explosion of the 1970's – locals having much more money to spend in the capital's shops.

The fire which swept through The Gran Hotel in 1994 remains shrouded in mystery, but the building has recently gone through a huge restructuring and is once again open as a five star hotel with amazing views from its top floor restaurant.

Today the city continues to be a thriving fishing and cargo port, as well as playing host to more and more cruise ships stopping en route across the Atlantic. El Reducto Beach must be one the few "inner city" beaches in the world, and there is a huge sports stadium in town which offers Canarian Wrestling, a full athletics set-up and is the home of our local football team UD Lanzarote, who are currently in the Spanish second division B.

The main shopping street (Calle Leon Y Castillo, but known locally as Calle Real) has been pedestrianised and has shops to suit every need and budget, and the seafront area to the west of the town has been transformed into a beautiful park for promenading. There is also a skate board park, and numerous children's play areas.

The man-made tidal lake known as El Charco is a great place to walk and has a number of restaurants and bars around its

27

perimeter. Night life is varied and interesting, reflecting the multi-cultural aspect of the city. There can't be many places in the world where you can find a Japanese Restaurant opposite a Tapas Bar and adjacent to a Pizza place!

Arrecife is certainly a modern and thriving city now, having endured many hardships over the years. But the old traditions remain: Early evening is promenading time, with whole families out for a stroll and a drink, you can regularly catch a game of Bolas at the end of the main road into town, and Sunday mornings are all about sailing model yachts in the harbour.

Haría

At the centre of the municipality, one finds the town of Haría, known locally as "The valley of a thousand palms." Legend has it that two palm tress were planted for each boy child born in the town, and one for each girl. The town is certainly the lushest area on the island, being in a valley which gathers any rainwater from the surrounding mountains.

The town came to prominence in the early 1900's, when the mayor Don Domingo Lopez Fontes sanctioned the design of the town centre, which remains as he intended today. There is a beautifully shaded square, planted with magnificent trees, which provides a delightful area to walk, or to enjoy a drink or meal.

The coast of the municipality features the town of Mala, which is full of the amazing Prickly Pear cactus fields. The plants were cultivated to provide an environment for the Cochineal Beetle, provider of a red dye used to colour both food and textiles. The dye was one of Lanzarote's major exports prior to tourism. Mala is also home to Chaco de Palo, a well known naturist resort.

Moving a little way north along the coast is the town of Arrieta, which has a superb sandy beach, as well as a long pier ideal for fishing. The bay here is great for snorkelling when calm, but safe for learning to surf when the waves are higher. The facilities on the beach are better than most, with showers, toilets and a small bar / restaurant. Visit Arrieta on a Sunday, and you will find the beach full of local families enjoying a swim and some Paella or tapas from the little bar.

28

Órzola is in the far north of Haría, and is a fishing village most famous for several fabulous fresh fish restaurants. The ferry to La Graciosa departs from here several times a day.

Haría boasts a high number of Lanzarote's best tourist attractions. Near Mala, there are the amazing cactus gardens, and a little way north one can find Los Jameos del Agua and La Cueva de los Verdes. The former is a tranquil testament to the skill of César Manrique and the latter is a spectacular volcanic cave system. The best view on the island is available at The Mirador del Rio, and exotic birds can be seen at Guinate Tropical Park.

A trip to Haría and its towns will soon dispel the myth that Lanzarote is a barren, volcanic rock – the gorgeous green scenery provides a wonderful contrast to our normal landscape.

Teguise

Teguise town was originally the capital of the island, and can be found almost in the centre of Lanzarote. As such the town was subjected to numerous invasions and sackings during the 15th and 16th century, which eventually lead to the building of the fort which now dominates the area.

The town is now best known for the splendid Sunday Market which is attended every week by thousands of locals and tourists. As well as local goods and produce the market offers a huge variety of purchases ranging from tacky "Lanzarote rock" to fake designer watches and sunglasses, but with some tasteful stuff as well!

The man-made resort of Costa Teguise has been built up dramatically over recent years and is now Lanzarote's second busiest resort area, with masses of bars, restaurants, shops and hotel and apartment complexes. The King of Spain has a magnificent holiday home there.

Also within the municipality, one can find Tahiche, where César Manrique once lived. His home is now the headquarters of the Foundation named in his memory and a spectacular place to visit, built over five volcanic bubbles.

29

Cutting across to the west will bring one to Tiagua, once a centre for growing high quality tobacco, and now a sleepy traditional village.

Tías

For many people the municipality of Tías is the most important on the island, with the main town being the fabulous resort of Puerto del Carmen.

Tías used to be called "Las Tías de Fajardo" or "The aunts of Fajardo" – this related to the two ladies who had a house in the area, Doñas Francisca and Hernan Fajardo, who were the aunts of Alonso Fajardo, once Governer of The Canaries. In recent times the name became shortened to its current version.

The town of Tías itself is set on the hill above Puerto del Carmen, and features some of the best views on the island. It is home to a thriving multi-national theatre and has some good restaurants and bars. From Tías, the villages of Conil and La Asomada boast some truly stunning villas set into the hillside.

Puerto del Carmen was once a simple fishing port, and the harbour remains intact in what is now known universally as "The Old Town." Tourism arrived here first in the 1970's, when entrepreneurs recognised the potential of the miles of sandy beaches and the potential for building lots of property within a few minutes walk of them. The first hotel built was Los Fariones, which remains one of the island's best places to stay. "The Strip" – the road which runs all along the seafront – now has many, many bars, restaurants and shops which offer a huge variety of music, tastes and duty-free bargains. The road runs for 5KM, with beach all along, and eventually merges with Matagorda near the airport. Puerto del Carmen is also the host town for the world famous Ironman competition, in which competitors swim, ride bikes and finally run a marathon along The Strip. Behind the main beach road, there are scores of apartment complexes and hotels, all designed and built in Lanzarote's inimitable low rise style.

A little way along the coast towards Playa Blanca, you will find Puerto Calero, which is fast becoming the yachting centre of The Canaries, and which plays host to some truly magnificent boats.

30

A five star hotel has recently opened, and Puerto Calero is also home to some of the island's best boat trips, ranging from jet skis to sailing catamarans, and the famous Yellow Submarine.

Tías provides a wonderful contrast within its borders, ranging from the thriving tourist centre at Carmen to the Million Euro mansions of La Asomada – it's no wonder that it remains the resort of choice for most people visiting Lanzarote.

Yaiza

The municipality of Yaiza offers some of the most beautiful and indeed, typical vistas of Lanzarote. The best place to view this area is from the mountain viewpoint at Femés. Looking to the right one can see the stunning Montañas del Fuego, scanning to the left one can spot the water spouts at Los Hervideros, followed by the green lagoon and salt pans at El Golfo. In the centre of the picture you will see the rapidly expanding resort of Playa Blanca, with Fuerteventura shimmering in the distance, and finally, all the way around to the right one will spot the beaches at Papagayo.

A trip down the new road from Yaiza will bring you into Playa Blanca, which was, until recently, a sleepy fishing village. In the past few years Playa Blanca has grown almost beyond recognition, with high class hotels and some of the most beautiful villas on the island sprouting up. A fabulous new marina has recently been completed, and there are plans for a number of golf courses on the plain around the town. The beaches at Papagayo are some of the best on Lanzarote, and can be reached via a long and sometimes rough track, but the uncomfortable trip is certainly worth it!

El Golfo provides one of the few black-sand beaches on the island, as well as being home to the amazing lagoon, which is set inside one half of a volcano – the other half having been eroded by the action of the sea. The vivid green colour is caused by a type of friendly bacteria.

Los Hervidores is found just beyond El Golfo, and is on the Northern coast of the island. A man-made path winds between the lava, and onto balconies jutting right over the sea. When the

31

tide or the wind is up, the sea crashes into holes on the lava rock, creating amazing water spouts.

Heading towards Yaiza, the views of Timanfaya (Las Montañas del Fuego) are unforgettable, with the changing colours of the sand reflecting the sunlight, and providing a stark contrast with the black volcanic lava.

Yaiza itself is so beautiful, it doesn't look real. Every house is so neat, the garden so perfect and the backdrop of the mountain provides a fantastic photographic canvas. At Christmas, Yaiza always produces the best nativity scene produced on the island, each year it seems to become more and more complex and detailed, but it always provides one of those "lump in the throat" moments.

Tinajo

The municipality of Tinajo is situated on the northern half of the island and encompasses the town of Tinajo, as well as the famous Famara beaches.

Historically it was always a difficult area for farmers due to the very sandy soil, but encouraged by the local priest who proved that crops could grow, using his own fields, the farmers cultivated the area intensively during the 17th century.

At the time of the volcanic eruptions in 1736, the local townspeople were terrified that the lava would engulf their now fertile land and their priest organised a procession to meet the lava flow and to invoke the help of the virgin to stop it. The crowd went to the very edge of the flow, planted a cross and prayed fervently that the flow should stop. They promised God that they would build a church on the spot if it should do so. The next day the lava turned away from the fields, and the people of Tinajo forgot their promise.

Many years later in 1774 a young goatherd, Juana Rafaela Acosta, was approached by a woman and told to let her parents know that if the church was not built as promised, the volcano would again erupt. She told her parents but they chided her for making up stories. The woman duly appeared again, this time leaving a "shadow" of her hand on the girl's shoulder. This time her parents took her to the church, where she identified the woman as The Virgin Nuestra Señora de los Dolores. The church was built and the virgin was proclaimed Señora de los Volcanes (Lady of the Volcanoes).

The town of Tinajo is thriving today, with some of the loveliest houses on the island. Driving down the hill takes one to the fabulous Famara Beach, which has spectacular cliffs hanging above golden sand. The surf here is legendary, but also very safe as the water is not deep.

Club La Santa is also in the municipality, and provides a wonderful venue for many top international athletes, as well as acting as main sponsor and host for the legendary Ironman Triathlon Competition.

San Bartolomé

San Bartolomé is the municipality most often forgotten when people are asked to name the different parts of the island. The municipality stretches from Playa Honda on the coast and travels inland through the town of San Bartolomé, encompassing Montaña Blanca and then peters out inland before Tinajo.

Amazingly, almost every visitor to Lanzarote passes through San Bartolomé, although few realise it. This is a function of the fact that the airport lies within its borders! The airport itself is a work of brilliant design. Despite having a runway long enough to permit Concord a visit (and yes she has been here) and despite handling a huge number of flights, the airport's low rise structure means it does not appear as a blot on the landscape. It is a delightful place for plane spotters, as a beach runs along the full length of the runway, allowing one to enjoy the sun as well as getting within 100 metres of aircraft taking off and landing. I have counted as many as 6 planes in the pattern at any one time, with two ready for take-off.

Moving to the North of the airport the first area one will find is Playa Honda. This is the residential and commercial heart of the island. Play Honda has a fabulous beach, with some excellent bars and restaurants right on the front, and a great deal of housing almost exclusively occupied by full-time residents. It's a good place for locals to escape the tourists for a few hours! As

33

one nears the circunvalacion the area becomes much more commercial, with The Deiland shopping centre, The Mega Centro department store, as well as numerous supermarkets and car showrooms. A visit to this area at the start of the evening shopping session often provides a rare experience for this island – a genuine traffic jam!

The inland part of San Bartolomé consists mainly of the town itself. This again is largely residential, and has expanded fast in recent years, offering easy access to Arrecife and Puerto del Carmen, whilst having the benefit of offering superb sea views due to its height.

Beyond the town the road to Tinajo is largely rural, with fields of sweet potatoes being very common. The local inhabitants were called Los Batateros (the sweet people) as a result, during the last century.

The only tourist attraction within the Municipality is the Monumento Al Campesino, which was placed at the exact centre of Lanzarote, by César Manrique, as a tribute to the working people of the island. The monument itself is an amazing design, and there is a museum which depicts life in rural Lanzarote before tourism. There is also a restaurant serving typical Canarian food. Well worth a visit!

The more Spanish parts of Lanzarote still adopt the traditional siesta system of breaking for a big lunch at one o'clock, then returning home for a sleep, going back to work for a few hours in the evening. We had a brief flirtation with siesta, but I really struggled to get back to work afterwards, and we soon adopted traditional British working hours. The siesta remains a much civilised luxury which we occasionally enjoy on a Sunday.........if the weather's not good enough for the boat or the beach!

So, having thoroughly researched the whole island, and armed with detailed knowledge of our new home, we set about working the business plan we had put so much time into on dark, cold nights in England.

34

Chapter Seven – OK, So The Business Doesn't Work!

You may remember that our plan was to provide a service for holiday makers visiting private villas on the island, and help them to make their stay more rewarding and comfortable. As part of this service, we went out and purchased a load of equipment, including baby seats, cots and fans, planning to rent them to our clients. The whole basis of the business was that property owners would be happy to pass on their client's details, so that we could contact them and sell ourselves. In return we would offer them a commission and the added benefit that the client would enjoy a better holiday and, therefore be more likely to come back again.

Our problem was one we hadn't anticipated. Most of the holiday rental property here is owned by people who live in Britain and Germany – we therefore really struggled to talk to the owners. We advertised locally, and we spent a lot of time and money putting leaflets into letter boxes, but it became apparent that we weren't talking to enough owners. Short of running massive adverts in British and German newspapers, which we couldn't afford, we weren't ever going to achieve our business objectives with the original plan.

Fortunately, the equipment hire side took off quite quickly, and we soon built up a reasonable little business out of that, with the products we bought quickly paying for themselves and moving into profit. We continued to offer the service for some years, when I finally became fed up with driving for two hours on a Sunday to deliver a couple of fans for a net profit of €38! We still get calls and pass all the leads on to what used to be our biggest competitor.

We were fortunate in still having a decent sum of money in the bank, but during this phase we could see it gradually dwindling. Our dilemma was that we were spending money fast on advertising and leaflets, but not seeing commensurate results. After several long discussions, we agreed that the original plan wasn't achievable and that we should continue to build the hire business, and look for other opportunities. We still believe that there is an opportunity here for our original idea, and that someone will eventually exploit it.

The best aspect of this early work is that it helped establish the name and logo of Estupendo, and most importantly it helped us to establish a style of business which we stick with to this day. Because the family were all in it together from day one, working from a small bungalow, the kids are involved with what we do. If you come to our offices in today, you might find Tia the dog, or one of the kids here, or indeed colleague's children. We don't wear business clothing, and we're quite happy to relax with a coffee with anyone who pops in, not just potential customers, but anyone who wants a natter. We don't ever do business with the many "dodgy" people on the island – Lanzarote is too small a place to let anyone down, and whilst our ethos is happy and relaxed (that's why we moved here) we always turn up to appointments on time, and always do our best for our clients. We don't want to be rich, just to earn a reasonable living and to sleep soundly at night. Our leisure time is much more important than it ever was, and we pack so much more into it than we ever did.

Chapter Eight - New Connection New Challenge

During our early days in Lanzarote there was a dearth of information and news available for the British community. There were no radio stations, and the venerable Holiday Gazette (a long running magazine aimed at Brits) was going through a particularly bad patch, recycling articles that weren't interesting the first time around. The Gazette has since had a total makeover and is a very interesting publication now.

We had been shopping and had noticed a newspaper called Island Connections on the shelves, which claimed to be the Canary Islands largest circulation English language publication. We bought the paper and enjoyed reading a mixture of national and international news written to a reasonable standard, although we immediately realised that there was no information at all on 'our' island. There was however a competition running asking for articles to be submitted for publication, with the prize being a meal for two. We decided it would be fun to enter and penned the following:

Published Island Connections 09/02/02 edition 407

Dear British Holiday Maker

It's wonderful to have you visit our island and to have you spend some of your hard earned money in our businesses. But, having emigrated from Britain some time ago, there are some things that puzzle me and amuse me about the way you behave on holiday, and I thought I'd share them with you:

1. *When you step off the kerb to cross the road looking in completely the wrong direction it causes my heart rate to double in a split second - please remember we drive on the right!*

2. *Whilst on the subject of driving. Despite the fact that it's in completely the wrong place, that really is a rear view mirror in the middle of the windscreen. Roundabouts are a nightmare here - just go for it! Despite the fact that locals never stop at them, there is no need for you to carry out an emergency stop*

37

every time someone gets within 5 feet of a pedestrian crossing.

3.   *I know that back home you dress conservatively and appropriately. Why is it that your dress sense goes completely out of the window just because you are in a warmer climate? Why is it that this affliction seems to particularly affect men over 35 with commensurately large beer bellies? Please remember that union jack shorts and sandals with socks were passe in the 20th century, and that hairy belly buttons have never been attractive. If men are able to survive 351 days a year without a handbag, why is it that you all carry an incredible assortment of rucksacks, shoulder bags and bum bags when here? On the subject of bum bags, surely "belly" bags would be a more appropriate name?*

4.   *You may notice on your travels that the pavements of Lanzarote can sometimes be narrow or indeed non-existent. Please remember that some of us have work to do, and cannot afford to wait patiently while you stop to admire the view or have a chat. We have tried to patent a baseball cap with built in wing mirrors, but perhaps an occasional glance over your shoulder will suffice.*

5.   *In common with other locals I have developed a cracking suntan, and you may mistake me for a Spaniard. This does not mean you can talk about me in English without me understanding every word you say.*

6.   *There are many places in Lanzarote which serve British beer together with British food, and show British sport on TV. If you return home from your holiday having failed to enjoy a genuine Tapas meal, or a drink in a bar where the menu isn't in pictures or English you may just have missed the point.*

7.   *When you are talking to Spanish people who don't understand you, increasing the volume and repeating the original sentence does not make any difference.*

8.   *We're tremendously lucky in having grown up licensing laws in Spain, which means we can drink anytime we want. A mid morning cognac with your coffee is cool - a pint of lager with your morning fry up isn't!*

9.   *The modern digital video camera is a wonderful tool. I'm sure the slow atmospheric pans across the stunning vistas seem like a great idea at the time, but I do ponder how many of you get home to view the tape and wonder "what was that all about?" And how many truly wonderful real life moments do you miss because you have one eye glued to the lens and most of your brain concentrated on achieving the correct white balance.*

10.   *We have pretty sensible parking rules here and the charges are both reasonable and clearly explained in English. Why is it then that so many of you seem to be competing to earn the highest number of parking tickets during your time here?*

I hope you won't be offended by my observations, if this isn't you I hope it's made you chuckle - if it is you I look forward to seeing you on the Avenida de las Playas!

We were delighted to be told that our article was to be published and that we had won a meal at the El Molino Blanco restaurant in Tenerife! Having no desire to visit Tenerife, much less pay a considerable sum of money to travel there for our 'free' meal, I decided to write to the editor. I explained my reasons for declining his kind offer, and also pointed out to him that as there was no information on Lanzarote in his newspaper I would refrain from buying any further copies.

A few days later my mobile phone rang and it was the man himself. He explained to me that he had been looking for someone to provide articles on Lanzarote and to sell advertising on the newspapers behalf. He asked me if I was interested, and suggested that I should put together some business ideas for him. So began a difficult, sometimes tempestuous, but always an interesting relationship.

39

Our original idea was to greatly increase circulation of the newspaper on the island by writing articles of interest to the people of Lanzarote. We also put together a whole series of suggestions for promoting Island Connections, on the grounds that if people were reading the newspaper they were far more likely to advertise in it. The editor was very keen on the former, but showed no interest in offering any financial support for the latter, and this remained a common theme in working with Sven Huesing. Despite working with Sven for more than a year I never met him and had perhaps two telephone conversations with him – all our dealings were via email. He has been described to me as extremely tall and very large; I do know that he is German and that he has lived on Tenerife for around 18 years. His Spanish business partner has been to Lanzarote and made us both laugh when we were discussing Sven's emails, which can be extremely abrupt. According to him, Sven is often very .... German!

The fortnightly newspaper runs to around 80 pages and is normally sold through supermarkets at €1.50. We were able to secure a regular free supply in order to get as many copies on to the streets as possible in the hope that once people were hooked they would continue to buy Island Connections. To hook them we came up with a series of ideas to fill what was initially one page on Lanzarote. Our main idea was to come up with a feature interview for every edition on an island 'celebrity'. This was born out of the fact that at every gathering of ex-pats one is inevitably asked 'How did you end up here?' 'Where are you from?' 'What did you do in the UK?' etc etc. We decided that we would pick on somebody for each edition and ask them the questions on behalf of the interested public. We were delighted at the response to this series and are proud that the newspaper has extended this idea to other islands, and that even the Holiday Gazette is now doing the same thing! We also wanted to provide information about local businesses and services and so we came up with the idea for a column called Business Connections.

In the early days our focus was on getting our 400 free papers out as quickly as possible. We soon established a network of businesses that were happy to stock the papers and I established a delivery round, using Speedy in order to reduce petrol costs and to aid parking. By using a combination of bungees and

40

rucksacks I was able to load 150 papers at a time on to Speedy, which I am sure resulted in the bike being way over its maximum safe weight. One of my delivery stops was the English butchers shop in Puerto del Carmen, Lanzameat, and I joked with Jim the owner one day that I was the oldest newspaper boy in Lanzarote. He immediately quipped back that he had been the oldest butcher's boy in Lanzarote for some time!

Our greatest success in terms of generating readers was a column called Lanzarote Lunches, where we wrote each fortnight a critique of a local restaurant. As well as being an extremely enjoyable way of discovering Spanish cuisine, we were also delighted at the number of people who followed our exploits into the culinary heartland of Lanzarote. We have been told that there are close to 2,000 restaurants on the island – to date we have covered just over 1% of the total but we do plan to keep at this task. One of the nicest stories we heard was about a couple from Gran Canaria who had come to Lanzarote for a holiday, and visited our local curry restaurant on the strength of the article that we had written. Steve's Balti House remained a loyal advertiser for years.

The hidden aspect of becoming instant journalists, and the one for which we remain eternally grateful, is the way in which the newspaper opened doors for us. We certainly didn't exploit this cynically, but it led to us meeting so many interesting people who in turn introduced us to their interesting friends. It also enabled us to establish a terrific reputation on the island for having the answers to other people's questions, and we have been able to offer help and advice to a lot of people as a result of our contacts.

Our first celebrity was the boxer Audley Harrison. A contact at Club La Santa called to let us know that Audley was in training there for an upcoming fight. I telephoned his agent who agreed to an interview the following Saturday, immediately after a personal appearance he was doing at Lineker's Sports Bar in Puerto del Carmen.

I arrived half an hour before the appointed time, to see a couple of Club La Santa liveried Golf Convertibles parked on the bus stop outside, with two Guardia officers talking earnestly into their radios. I ran in to Lineker's, hurriedly introduced myself to

41

Audley and his team, and told them about the problem. Now Audley is very, very big and very, very black. His "minders" were even bigger! They all wore white tracksuits adored with massive gold chains and rings. I swear I saw the Guardia cop shiver when he turned to see them approaching, with me close behind. The conversation, with me translating went something like this:

"We've called the trucks to tow your cars away, as you're parked on a bus stop."

"I'm really sorry, officer, we'll move them right now for you."

"Well I can cancel the truck, but you need to pay a fine of €120."

"OK, give me a ticket and I'll get my people to deal with it."

"Pay now, in cash, or we tow them away." This with arms defensively folded.

"I don't have any cash on me, my people will sort this out."

"Well they'll have to collect the cars from the pound, and the fine will be €400 then."

At this point, Audley checked his pocket and found a credit card – he then ran across the road to a cashpoint – whilst he was there, I pointed out to the cop that he was dealing with the Olympic heavyweight champion, but he professed to never having heard of him, but he did whisper to me that he was an extremely large coño! Audley returned with the readies and at that point both officers became extremely amiable and asked for an autograph and a photo with the great man.

I actually conducted the interview on the street, with passers by shouting "Alright Audley!" at frequent interviews. The finished product was not something I was particularly proud of, and I have to admit that I'm simply not good at getting past the standard platitudes that celebrities seem to conjure up in answer to my prepared questions. Parkinson makes it look so easy!

While we were building up our readership and advertisers, income from the newspaper was appalling, so we decided that we should look for some kind of "real" work. Julie very quickly got herself a job in the accounts department of a large resort hotel – a real result, as it was well paid and came with a full contract and social security payments. She stayed there for a total of three years and provided a fantastic financial bedrock for the family whilst I worked at various business ideas. During this time she made numerous friends, with incredibly diverse

42

nationalities. As our own company Estupendo became more successful, she gradually reduced her hours with the resort, and eventually the day came when she could join us full time.

Shortly after she had started I was contacted by an advertiser, a new estate agency on the islands, and asked if I would like to help them to build up a property portfolio. I explained that I had no experience in estate agency, but Geoff the manager told me that he needed someone who had lots of contacts, and that the company would provide full training. He also agreed that he would be flexible enough to allow me to continue to build up both Estupendo and the newspaper business. So, six months after landing here, we both had contracts with basic salaries, which meant that the financial pressure was finally off. I remained with Interealty for exactly a year, and I did indeed create a large and diverse portfolio for them. But the best aspect of my time there was that it sowed the seeds for the business that Estupendo eventually became – but that story is several chapters away! Let's return to Island Connections and that period in our lives here.

Without doubt the high point in our journalistic career was when we managed to secure an interview with Bertie Ahern, the Irish Prime Minister.

It was a Thursday morning and I was busy working at the estate agent's when Julie took the call. She was on a day off, and the editor of our newspaper called to say that she had received a tip-off from a major Irish Newspaper that Bertie Ahern was holidaying on the island. She went on to say that Ahern is notoriously press-shy, especially when on holiday, so there was no chance of an interview, but the Irish paper would pay "Big bucks" for a photo of Ahern in relaxed holiday mood. Unsure of what to do, Julie asked the editor's advice. She suggested that we hung around outside the hotel and tried to catch him with a paparazzi-type shot.

She checked the web for pictures of him to be sure that she'd recognise him if he appeared, and headed off to Los Fariones Hotel in Puerto Del Carmen. She'd been there about an hour when she called me and said she was really uncomfortable with the whole thing. After some discussion we agreed that paparazzi shots weren't our style, and that even Prime Ministers were entitled to some peace on our little slice of paradise.

That evening we sent an e-mail to our editor explaining what we had done and why, and within minutes the phone rang. She told us that the Irish paper were very serious and reiterated that they wanted to pay a lot of money. After some discussion we decided that the only way we would progress this was via a direct approach. So we wrote a note to Ahern:

Thursday

Dear Mr Ahern,

Welcome to Lanzarote. We run the Lanzarote pages of the local Canarian newspaper Island Connections.

If you are able to spare any time for a quick photograph and perhaps a few words for our many Irish readers we would be very grateful.

Our only celebrity so far has been Audley Harrison, who visited three month's ago – it would be wonderful to have a political heavyweight!

We fully understand if you are unable to do this, and wish you a wonderful stay here. Hopefully the weather will improve, this cloud is very unusual!

Kind Regards,

Julie and Mike Cliffe-Jones

We dropped the note, with a business card and a copy of our newspaper in at reception on the Friday morning and returned home.

Within an hour the telephone rang and it was the PM's press secretary, who told us to call the following evening after six, saying that Mr Ahern would give us a few minutes. After the shock subsided, we called our editor to tell her that we would

44

have the story and she duly passed this on the Dublin, where they decided to literally hold the presses for their Sunday edition, awaiting the arrival of our photographs.

The following day dragged on and on, until the appointed time – I made the call, and our contact told us to be in the hotel reception in 20 minutes. On the journey down, I began to really suffer from nerves, realising that this was grown-up stuff, and that I was not actually a journalist at all.

The hotel reception is plush and old fashioned and I suddenly felt very underdressed for the occasion, wearing my surf type trousers, trainers and tee-shirt. Bertie Ahern strode through the milling crowd, security man in tow, and beamed a smile that only Irish people seem to be able to do. Pausing en route to say hello to someone very senior from RTE, he lead us to a quiet corner of the foyer, and gave us his full attention. The interview is recorded in full for posterity, both in Island Connections, and on my office wall, so I won't bore you with the details here, but Ahern was charming. He answered all of our questions, was very complementary about Lanzarote, and even joked with Julie about her broken arm. After our chat I asked him if we could take some photographs around the swimming pool area, and he immediately agreed. I set up the pose just in front of a dying sun, and next to a beautifully lit palm tree and was just about to press the shutter button when he said: "Just one thing, Mike – these photos are for your newspaper *only*, no other publication." Just to be sure I checked "Just for us? No other publication?" "Correct, he responded, that's the deal." I agreed and got the shots, sweat breaking out on my brow and with a mental picture of the massive presses in Dublin waiting idly, surrounded by hundreds of print workers tapping their fingers. We said our good byes, thanking "Bertie" for his time, and wandered toward the car in a daze.

Without discussing it we knew what we had to do, and Julie called Dublin. She explained that Ahern had been very specific and that we had agreed not to publish the photos elsewhere. Our contact in Dublin then offered a large sum of money for each photo, and we declined. There then followed an amazing series of calls, with the price going up all the time. We explained that we had given our word and that the answer was still no. The Dublin paper asked what we needed to send them the photos, and

45

we said Bertie Ahern's approval, so they said they'd contact him at the hotel. What happened next was very strange. My phone rang and an Irish lady identified herself as "A journalist" on the island. She said she had heard that we had photos of Ahern and that she would like to buy the negatives. With my mind in a whirl I told her that they were not for sale, but when I subsequently checked the number on my phone I realised that the call had come from Ahern's hotel, so I can only assume that it was someone from his party checking that I was keeping my word.

In the end the Dublin paper ran an "Ahern on Holiday in Lanzarote" story without our pictures and our article and photos duly appeared in the next edition of Island Connections as an exclusive. IC make no differentiation over the content of articles when it comes to paying, so our exclusive with a serving Prime Minister earned us the princely sum of €29.58, which didn't even cover the cost of the calls to Dublin. But then, there can't be many people in the world who can slip the words "When I met the Irish Prime Minister..........." into a conversation!

We worked extremely hard with Island Connections, and eventually we had three full pages devoted to Lanzarote, with a commensurate amount of advertising. But it eventually began to dawn on us that the money we were making from the writing and sales simply didn't warrant the hours we were putting in.

I had a look at a web site the other day which acts a resource for freelance writers working in Spain, and it offered the following advice: 'Don't ever imagine that you will make a living writing for local newspapers in the Spanish islands, it simply doesn't pay enough.' It took us many months to realise the truth of this, but we eventually told Sven that he should seek another team for Lanzarote. We continued to write the articles for six or seven months, and eventually handed control over to another ex-pat. The whole thing was a wonderful experience and I wouldn't change a single moment of it.

Chapter Nine – Opening Doors

So, at this point in our story, we had both settled into contracted jobs, Julie with the resort and me at the estate agents. Estupendo was running quietly away in the background as an equipment hire company and we were still in our rented bungalow in Puerto del Carmen.

Tia the dog had settled in superbly, she had become firm friends with all our neighbours and spent most of the day sleeping in the shade of our palm trees, looking forward to the next walk. The only dog related problem we have encountered here is the little spiky seeds of cactus plants, which embed themselves in dog's paws. Julie has a little ritual which Tia seems to enjoy – after every walk, she lies on her back (Tia, that is!) and Julie picks the little balls out of her feet. Some vets do offer a service where they spray silicon onto the dog's paws, but this has always struck me as a bit strange.

Lucy was thriving at the British School, which we quickly discovered favours kids who are real achievers. She was doing well academically, and was really developing into a great sports star, playing in the football team and representing the school as a middle distance runner. Lucy had been a small, quite asthmatic child in UK, but had now developed into a strong, tanned, fit young lady – a wonderful advert for our new lifestyle. We went and watched her run in a huge competition is the main Arrecife stadium, and then she was selected for a cross Canarian event in Gran Canaria. After years of watching the kids go to sports events in an old bus, it seemed strange to drop Lucy at the airport for the flight. She came back with medals and some great photos of our neighbouring island.

Josh, on the other hand, wasn't getting the best from the school. He's a bright enough lad, but, like so many teenage boys, he isn't exactly motivated. I blame the school to some extent, as they do seem to focus on pushing as fast as possible, to get the best from the hardest working kids, often leaving many behind.

Two further things were a concern for us during this time, one was that neither Josh nor Lucy were learning Spanish fast enough. Colegio Hispano Britanico make sure that every child does at least 40 minutes of Spanish each day, so the kids get a basic understanding. But as all of the teachers and most of the pupils are Brits, English is spoken all the time. We felt strongly that, if Josh and Lucy chose to make their home here in the future, they would have to speak Spanish like natives. The other bug bear was the cost of the school. When you're looking at the price of private school here from the basis of a UK salary, it can seem relatively cheap, but once you start earning a Canarian wage, the fees are enormous, and it seems that every exam taken and every school trip required more money. We deferred any decisions about education to the future, but it was beginning to play on our minds.

We were also beginning to look at where we lived – we still faced the problem that there were too many of us in a small bungalow, and we had realised that the problem with living in a resort is that your neighbours seem to change every couple of weeks, making long term friendships extremely difficult!

However, one thing that staggers me about this island is the diversity of people who live here and we were soon travelling the island meeting new friends from every walk of life and a huge range of nations.

An example was a friendship we established with the German community early on. Both Josh and Lucy were friends with two brothers at their school, Alexander and Fabian, and they were invited to a birthday party in Teguise. This being the first birthday party since our arrival, I hadn't realised that it is an all day event catering for the children and their accompanying parents. We arrived expecting as you do in the UK - spend a couple of minutes with the pleasantries, drop the kids and run to luxuriate in the time until one has to return to collect one's offspring. Walking into the garden we met a mixed group of German and Spanish adults and, having been abandoned by Josh and Lucy, we were a little lost as to what to do next. Andrea emerged from the group and introduced herself as Alexander and Fabian's Mum. She encouraged us to go and enjoy ourselves for a few hours, and then return to either collect the children or come back and join the party in the evening. We left the house not knowing what to do about later, we hadn't seen or heard any other English people and our German was limited to Auf Wiedersehn Pet!

48

We spent an enjoyable afternoon on the beach, and decided that we should return with a bottle of tinto for the evening session. We arrived at the house to find the children lighting a bonfire on the common land outside and the adults sitting round the table inside. Andrea welcomed us and sat us down with the group introducing us to her partner Jurgen and close friends Hans and Lisa. There was delicious home made chilli and a local delicacy of sweet golfio balls with plenty of red wine. I found that the time passed really quickly, I was amazed to find that we could converse with the group in a mixture of German, Spanish and English with energetic hand movements to illustrate any difficult words.

Apart from the birthday, it was also a local fiesta of San Juan when bundles of straw are set alight and rolled down the hills. Luckily the landscape is barren so it does not ignite or the local bomberos would be busy dousing the flames. The tradition is combined with jumping the bonfires and as terrifying as this sounded the children were insisting that they had to try it. Luckily they were persuaded to make smaller separate bonfires that they were able to jump, this did not stop my heart from being in my mouth as one slip meant that a child would be burnt. The German tradition was for the birthday presents to be opened at Midnight so it was early morning before we bundled into the car and headed down the hill towards home.

Sadly our newly found friends announced some months later that they were returning to Germany. Andrea told us that she had talked to Alexander and Fabian and they missed Germany – mainly the snow in the winter which is one thing you definitely do not expect to find in Lanzarote. Her business was not doing as well as she had expected and thought after four years here maybe the time was right to head home.

Hans and Lisa remain friends to this day, and we have established many other friends with German people, helped by the fact that we now live in the north.

Another thing that is interesting here is that the class system doesn't seem to exist. At any given gathering, there can be a terrific mixture of people, from wealthy retired diplomats to

49

humble cockney cleaners, not something that seems to happen back in England.

We also met some really interesting characters in those early days. One that stands out in my mind was Anthony Harrison.

At the time we met him, Anthony had been on the island for nearly 20 years. Together with his friends Eric and Sam he purchased a beautiful house at Guime where he lived with his menagerie of 6 dogs and 10 cats. The three, together with Eric's brother John became great friends in the UK running a china and glass business in Surrey. Anthony had previously been in the hotel business, getting out when Trust House Forte Group took his hotel over. The lads decided on Lanzarote both to enjoy our fabulous weather and to get away from the punishing tax regime in the UK.

Anthony's earliest recollections of Lanzarote revolved around witnessing a great deal of cruelty to animals and the number of stray dogs and cats roaming the island at that time. This led to the hombres becoming involved with PALS having been introduced to their next door neighbour who was president. At that time PALS was a totally unofficial organisation that simply did what it could to help animals in need. PALS has now evolved into the organisation NEW PALS which is made up of a committee and some 150 members. The organisation holds a regular monthly jumble sale on the last Saturday of each month from 10.30 am at Guime Social Club, together with a twice yearly auction. These, combined with 50 collection boxes sited all over the island help NEW PALS to fund their neutering programme, their 5 kennels and a relocation programme. Cats on many of the island's tourist complexes are neutered and spayed whilst the dogs are chipped and vaccinated then cared for in the kennels until they can be found a new home. Anthony is proud of a special relationship with Germany where many of the dogs are re-housed. Chris and Julie run the kennels which are located on the Playa Honda – Guime road. They are always looking for people with a little time to spare to walk the dogs. NEW PALS is always looking for good quality jumble, and we can recommend the jumble sales both as an opportunity to grab a bargain and also as a great social function.

Anthony could be regularly heard on one of Lanzarote's radio stations – UK Away FM, and his radio career dated back to his early days on the island when he acted as Technical Assistant for his friend Eric's Volcanic Island Discs programme. Eric Corrie was a well known UK actor who made his mark here on both Radio Litoral, Radio Volcan and Televolcan. Sadly both Eric and John died before we met Anthony, but he had no bitterness, and simply threw himself into his charity work. He could be seen chain smoking in his ancient battered Citroen van, whilst screaming around collecting jumble.

I remember one day enjoying a drink from his balcony. The view from the house was simply stunning, with the whole coast from Puerto del Carmen to Arrecife clearly visible. The airport looked like a child's toy set and when I commented upon it to Anthony, he recalled the day in November 1999 when he was walking the dogs on Playa Honda beach and witnessed Concorde lifting into the sky, with the after burners streaming fire as she rose from the end of the runway.

Through NEW PALS and his other activities, Anthony enjoyed a tremendous social life on the island, and indeed seemed to know everybody. As we were leaving his house once, we were introduced to Sir Ernest Hall, the industrial entrepreneur and patron of the arts.

Anthony joined Eric and John towards the end of 2004 after a short illness, his legacy is the thriving organisation New Pals has become, and the warm memories that so many islanders have of him.

Chapter Ten Settled At Last, and We're Ready to Move!

So, having been here a year, we had settled into a nice routine. We were making ends meet and above all we had established the new lifestyle we had so earnestly sought, spending more time with the kids and enjoying the fabulous ocean all around us. But Puerto del Carmen was beginning to grate on us.

The area we were in was beautiful, but it had two major drawbacks – first it was very English, and that frustrated us, having been so determined to become much more Spanish, and secondly, because we were in a holiday- let area, it was difficult to make friends locally, as they were only ever around for a couple of weeks. The reality was that although we were living in Carmen, we were actually spending all our time in either Arrecife, or on the beaches in the North of the island. So we decided it was time to move.

Our biggest problem at that time was budget. We needed at least three bedrooms, and really wanted a fourth as we were running the business from home. But at that time our earnings were pretty low. It gradually dawned on us that the answer was to move to Arrecife, which still provides the lowest cost accommodation on the island, as well as being totally Spanish – something we were really seeking.

As an aside, during this period I received a call at the estate agency asking me to value some new build properties in a little village in the north of the island called Punta Mujeres. I duly arranged to meet the constructor, and was surprised when I was introduced to a young, slim, English lady called Michelle Braddock. She and her husband Tila had bought a plot of land in the village and had just started construction on six houses. Viewing the site, I fell in love with both the village and the houses, and hoped one day to buy somewhere similar. I couldn't know it at the time, but almost two years later, we were to buy one of the six houses. But that was some way off.

Lanzarote is a pretty old fashioned place, and most things are passed on by word of mouth. So we really struggled to find places for rent advertised in Arrecife. Eventually, we were given the name of a lady who worked at the airport, and who could find

52

property. We told her what we were looking for, and she immediately booked for me to go and view an apartment near the sports stadium. She had told me the rent was just 540 Euros per month, and I was astonished to discover that it was a piso (a whole floor of an apartment building), and that there were four large bedrooms, two bathrooms, an enormous separate kitchen, and front and rear balconies, with sea views to the back. I duly arranged to take Julie and the kids to view, and we unanimously agreed that it would be a great place to live. The owners of the building lived downstairs, and the agent introduced me as an English writer (I was writing for the newspaper still at that time), and I'm convinced they thought I was some kind of celebrity.

Having decided to go for it, we struggled hard to cover the two month's deposit, as well as the agent's fee of nearly 1000 euros, but over a couple of weeks we managed to make all the payments to her. The owners put all new furniture in for us, and we moved in with our little Saxo over a couple of days. There were 69 steps up to our apartment, and I got to know every single one intimately during the move!

Arrecife life suited us really well. We were just 10 minutes walk from the main shopping areas, and we loved the little bars and cafes which are everywhere. It was a real luxury to be able to order pizza to be delivered, and we met Martin and Yenise, who remain friends to this day.

Almost 30% of the population of Arrecife is South American, with people from Brazil, Argentina, Colombia and Peru. They come here, of course, because the language is theirs. Martin and Yenise were from Argentina, and they ran a bar in Arrecife called Goa. They are an ambitious couple, and they had started to learn some English before we met. But our arrival prompted a terrific deal – we would teach them English, if they would teach us Spanish. There followed many nights, usually eating one of Martin's amazing curry pizzas (you have to try it) with us speaking to them in bad Spanish, and them replying in pretty poor English. It caused great confusion to other customers, but did us both a power of good. We also learned the differences, which are quite marked, between *our* Spanish and *South American* Spanish.

53

During our time in Arrecife, the work to revamp the city was just starting, and the Cabildo has done a magnificent job. El Reducto beach is fabulous, and how many capital cities in the world can boast a huge sandy beach within 5 minutes of the main shopping street? It was also a joy to shop in Arrecife, as everything is so much cheaper than in the resorts, and by touring all the side streets, there are some really excellent clothes and furniture shops to be found.

For the first time we had some real space to live in. Both kids really enjoyed having large, separate bedrooms and I particularly relished having my own office, and a decent sized kitchen to work in. We spent many hours experimenting with trying to replicate tapas recipes. Above all, we were really getting into the Spanish way of life. Saturday mornings were for getting up late, and enjoying a croissant, freshly squeezed juice and a coffee at our favourite restaurant, followed by some household or food shopping. We discovered a little line of shops around the corner from our apartment, where there was a greengrocer, a fish shop and a butchers. All these provided wonderful food and at remarkably cheap prices. We'd often then enjoy lunch at El Charco de San Gines, which is a tidal lake in Arrecife, surrounded by wonderful fish restaurants.

It was during this time that I had my first flirtation with the idea of siestas. Almost all of the businesses and shops in Arrecife still follow siesta, closing at around 1 in the afternoon and reopening from 5 until 8 in the evening. Adopting a "When in Rome......" attitude, I decided to try this out. But try as I might, I really struggled to get motivated to work again after a long break in the afternoon. I continue to envy my Spanish friends, who are able to enjoy a cracking lunch with wine and beer, go home to sleep for an hour, and return to work for the evening shift. For us, siesta is now an occasional weekend treat, and I've come to the conclusion that it simply doesn't suit the northern European constitution.

Looking back, I feel that the time in Arrecife was the making of us – we were forced to integrate into a Spanish way of life, we learnt so much more about our new kinfolk, and we got to know the capital in great detail. We still enjoy shopping in Arrecife almost every week, and we have an intimate knowledge of where to go for whatever we want. Of course our Spanish improved greatly, and little milestones like ordering a pizza by telephone for the first time, or asking a butcher to mince some steak, remain treasured memories.

On Sundays we joined the great throng leaving the city, and headed for the beaches. Arrieta became our favourite, and we would spend all day surfing or snorkelling (depending on conditions), enjoying a beer and a tapa at lunchtime, then head to our favourite restaurant for a bite at the end of the day, El Almacer is a terrific place, which opens from 5 until 8 each evening. There is a balcony which hangs over the sea and it serves some of the best seafood on the island. One of the best features is that they steadfastly refuse to offer the standard children's options of chicken nuggets, slice of pizza etc. What they give to kids is anything on the adult menu, served in a half portion. As in most traditional Spanish restaurants children are not ignored by the staff, they are treated as part of the party and every effort is made to make the experience as enjoyable for them as for the adults. They eat the same food, they can enjoy a glass of beer or wine, and they are as much a part of the conversation as any adult at the table. This does wonders for their social skills, and this really shows up when visiting friends in UK, where kids are expected to keep quiet and eat the chicken nuggets while the adults talk. This is an aspect of our lives of which I am particularly proud – whether it is just the four of us, or we are a party of twenty, I can rely on Josh and Lucy to contribute to the conversation and enjoyment at any social occasion, as can most Spanish children.

One of our funniest experiences occurred during our first Christmas in Arrecife. As usual, we had celebrated Christmas day on the beach, and we were looking forward to King's Day (6th January), which is when the Spanish children receive their presents. It was New Year's Eve and we decided we would celebrate in style now we were in "The City". We had learned that everything happens much later in Spain, so our plan was to have a really nice meal and head out into town, with the kids, at around 11PM. Having received Jamie Oliver's latest cook book as a present, Lucy and I decided we would cook a carpachio of beef for the family. Everyone really enjoyed the meal, which we served with shavings of fresh parmesan, a huge salad and a mustard dressing, and we then put on some fairly smart clothes on and headed for the main night spots along the seafront.

55

As we walked, it gradually began to dawn on me that there was something wrong. Instead of the expected hoards of partying revellers, there was an eerie silence over the whole city and every bar was closed. It was like a ghost town, the only sound coming from behind closed doors, where the scrape of knives and forks suggested everyone was at home enjoying a meal. As midnight approached, I became frantic at the thought of wishing each other a happy new year without even a bottle of water for a toast. We finally found a single place open, La Cerveceria, the only real tourist bar in Arrecife, and we sat down with a few German and British tourists to see the New Year in. The staff made a token effort, giving out party hats and treats and we waited for the blaring television to begin the countdown. I was despondent; having been convinced that this would be a new year's to remember, but smiled and kissed along with everyone else. And then the most amazing thing happened – seconds after midnight had struck, lights went on, all the bars opened, and out of every apartment building and house people, in full evening wear, burst onto the streets. This was all accompanied by a magnificent firework display. From being a damp squib, the party turned into one of our best ever. We walked round to Goa later, and spent a fabulous few hours with Martin and Yenise, staying up until 4.30AM. They explained that the tradition is for everybody to enjoy a meal with their families until midnight, when everyone eats the traditional 12 grapes as the chimes strike, and then the party begins. We felt decidedly underdressed that first night, but we have learnt our lesson well, and now we follow the traditional approach to New Year's with all our friends.

Chapter 11 – The Demise of Speedy

Whilst in Arrecife, we continued to use Speedy, the Aprilia scooter, as a secondary means of transport, and it proved brilliant to park around the city. The problem was, my work with the British estate agency required me to use the car more and more, and as a consequence Julie started using Speedy to get to and from her work in Costa Teguise.

I had been nervous about Julie riding Speedy, but she insisted that she didn't drive like a girl and would be just fine; after all it was only 10 minutes down the road. I had insisted on taking her to a quiet spot the Sunday before to show her how to start it etc, the hardest part for her had seemed to be pulling the bike on its stand. I was still worried; Julie had only driven cars before apart from our quad bike trek earlier in the year.

For the first few days I made her call me when she had arrived at the resort, and I would meet her if it was dark on her way back. After a couple of days I started to relax, after all she was a competent driver, what was I worried about? I asked Julie how she was finding it and she said the worst part was starting out from home with the workmen from the building site jeering and shouting comments at her.

We had been in our apartment for several months when Julie's Mum called and asked if could she come and stay for a week. The visit was well timed as Christmas was around the corner, Jenny would be able to see our new home as well as playing Mrs Santa Claus delivering the presents from the UK and taking ours back with her.

On the day of Jenny's arrival Julie was working so I had picked up her Mum from the airport and settled her into the apartment, the kids had arrived back from school and we were just waiting for Julie to come home before going out for a meal. Julie rang to say she was leaving and would see me in 15 minutes, although it was nearly half an hour later when she walked through the door.

Julie greeted her Mum and excused herself and went to the bathroom, this didn't surprise me as she is always bursting for the loo when she arrives home. It was a few minutes later when

57

she stuck her head round the corner of the office and said "I'm ok, I had an accident on the way home but don't tell Mum!" At this point her Mum was just next door so with my heart in my mouth and feeling dreadfully sick I whispered "What happened?" She proceeded to tell me that a car had pulled in front of her a few minutes from home, she had braked hard causing the wheels to lock and the next thing she remembered was scraping along the road with the bike skidding next to her. Not able to breathe properly as she had bruised her ribs Julie had stood up, brushed herself off and looked round to find several worried onlookers jabbering away in Spanish. Blurting out odd words along the lines of vale, gracias, ok, no policia, vivo en Arrecife etc only had the audience even more concerned, they wanted to call for the police and an ambulance. Someone had stood the bike back up so as Julie had got her breath back she jumped on it. Luckily it started and she wobbled off down the street, ashamed and wondering how she was going to arrive home and get away with this.

So no-one else was any the wiser, Julie didn't look like she'd had an accident despite wearing ¾ length trousers and open toed sandals. She had cleaned up her bleeding knees and told me that her arm was painful but just sprained. The following day she had the office Christmas lunch which consisted of swapping presents for everyone and Pot Luck, which is meant to be your speciality dish that you prepare and take in. As organised as ever she had not bought any of the presents or decided what she was cooking, so we set out for a shopping trip and a meal with Mum. As we left the building Julie diverted attention away from the bike and I tried very hard not to look for signs of her accident. Luckily Josh didn't notice the scrapes on the carbon fibre body and torn off stickers, but it made me feel sick. I kept looking at Julie who was trying so hard to be 'normal' with her Mum. She had tucked her sprained arm in the pocket of her coat and didn't look too bad considering. It became apparent as we shopped that something was wrong, as we purchased more and more items the bags were filling up and she was only using her left arm. Still convinced that her Mum wouldn't have noticed she said nothing and we went for our meal. We were greeted at Goa like long lost friends and we introduced Jenny and subsequently had a lovely meal (Julie struggling to eat pasta and drink cerveza left handed).

58

It was on the walk home that Julie mentioned to her Mum that she had crashed my beloved Speedy on her way home and she finally admitted that she had actually hurt herself. When we got back we had a good look at her arm and strapped it up in a sling whilst we got on with preparing the food required for the office party the next day. Julie wrapped up the presents as best as she could – not the easiest job left handed.

A few hours later we bade each other goodnight and we retired to the bedroom. Julie couldn't lift her arm properly to take off her clothes and decided that she had better get it checked out at the hospital. Leaving Mum in charge of the children we headed off for our first encounter with the emergency department at the city hospital. On the way over it dawned on us that we hadn't reported the moped accident and maybe we shouldn't say that's how the injury happened so we explained that it was a bike accident and we didn't correct them when it was assumed to be a bicycle! At the hospital we were checked in, luckily Julie had got her work card in the October so we had the right documents for treatment. I was told to stay in the waiting room whilst she was whisked off through a private door. I wanted to go with her but the Spanish custom is that the whole family accompanies the patient to the hospital whenever anyone is ill. Therefore, so that the treatment areas do not get congested, they are not permitted beyond the waiting room. I waited in this room, with at least five people for every other patient. Their moods ranged from indifferent to wailing agony.

It seemed like forever but Julie had only been an hour when she walked back through the door. Relief washed over me, her arm was strapped in a professional Velcro sling and she smiled saying "I've had an x-ray and it's sprained, but they want me to see a specialist in the morning", we headed home and to bed as it was nearly two in the morning, unfortunately for Julie we were out of pain killers and she spent a very uncomfortable night with not much sleep.

The next morning she rang the office and said she would see them later as she had a hospital appointment first. I dropped her off at the hospital and headed in to work, I had just reached my office 20 minutes later when the mobile went and she said "I've been plastered can you come and pick me up!" I was amazed to see Julie waiting outside with the biggest full arm cast I've ever

59

seen, her arm was bent across her chest and in plaster from her fingers to her shoulder. She explained that the specialist had said to her that her arm was broken; when she questioned this he squeezed her lower arm and when she screamed he said "See, it's broken!" He had then manipulated and plastered her arm in the space of 10 minutes and booked a follow up appointment for 2 weeks later at the local hospital.

I took her home to show her Mum, and then she promptly said "Can you drop me in the office with the presents and food please?" I insisted on coming in to see their reaction; she was really embarrassed as she hates any comments on women drivers and despises criticism where her driving is concerned. The girls were amazed to see her in and we both wondered how she would manage with her job for the next few weeks. She soon adapted to writing and typing with her left hand, to the point where she insisted on writing the family's Christmas cards even though it looked like a primary school child had written them.

In a fit of macho pique I decided that Speedy had to go, and that we needed to get back to being a two car family. At this time our other car was still the little Citroen Saxo, which had served us so well, but which I struggled with as it didn't have air conditioning. We decided to visit Pablo, our friendly bank manager and venture into the world of Spanish consumer credit. Pablo and Solbank were very accommodating, and we headed out looking for two decent second hand cars, with a reasonable sum of money. Now, you might recall Luis, owner of Bordon Automoviles in Arrecife, who sold us both our first car and also Speedy. Luis is probably the world's greatest salesman – all slicked back hair and soft voice, and we decided early in our search that we would avoid going to him as we would inevitably end up doing the wrong thing.

Our brief was simple – we wanted one new or almost new hatchback for me to use for work (with aircon) and something cheap and cheerful for Julie to get to and from the office. Over a period of a week we visited every outlet on the island, and they just couldn't offer us what we wanted, even when confronted with the opportunity to sell two cars. The other problem we had was that we had advertised Speedy everywhere, and we weren't getting any calls. In desperation, one Saturday, and accompanied by Josh, we sneaked in to Luis's showroom to see what he had,

60

hoping he wouldn't be in. The coast seemed clear and I quickly raced around the cars on display, looking at mileages and prices. My heart stopped when I heard his dulcet tones: "¿Señor Cliffe, que tal?" "Hola Luis, todo bien gracias, y tu?" And we were off and running! I explained our predicament to him, and he soothingly sat us down. He quickly grasped the situation, and said he would trade speedy in (for almost what we paid) and sort us out a couple of suitable cars. Indeed he had the perfect car for Julie already – a nice little Seat Marbella. "Let's go and have a look." He said and we headed off to his yard. Now, there is no way Luis could have known we were coming in, but looking back, I had set myself up perfectly. As we rounded the corner to the yard we were confronted by a simply gorgeous Fiat Bravo GT, in bright yellow, with huge alloys and an enormous sports exhaust. You couldn't miss this car – it dominated the display in every way. Josh's first reaction was "Cooooooooooool!" Mine was "Oh Sh*t!". Luis glided over to a pretty nice light blue Marbella, which he opened and started for us. Josh was drooling over the Fiat, and I was being continually distracted by the sight of it. It was obvious that the Marbella was just right for us, and we quickly agreed a deal on it. Luis then suggested we headed back for the showroom, so that he could begin the search for my new car. As we passed the Fiat, he hesitated, and took the keys out of his pocket "to show the boy". I couldn't help myself, I peered in and clocked the ten disc CD changer, the electric everything and the full climate control. Once again, as I had done a couple of year's previously, I asked Luis "How much is this one?" And once again, we ended up doing a deal on the Fiat, with the Marbella "thrown in". I really enjoyed that car while we had it, it was the only one of that spec on the island, and it really attracted attention. It was fast enough and handled really well, but was blighted by poor reliability, and a huge thirst for very expensive front tyres.

I enjoyed the Fiat for a year or so, and eventually replaced it with a new, and eminently more practical car, but the Marbella remained with us for years. Christened Bella, our little Sea never missed a beat, and seemed to consistently cost less than €100 a year to service and repair.

Luis remains a "Hello, how are you doing?" friend who we visit from time to time in Arrecife, and we continue to recommend him to newcomers.

Chapter 12 – Estupendo Becomes a Real Company

I should recap on where we were business wise at this point. Julie was still working full time at the resort hotel, and I was still working on my contract with the estate agency, bringing new properties in for them to sell. We had handed the newspaper over to the new incumbent, and Estupendo was ticking along nicely as an equipment hire company, and we were both working on that during evenings and weekends.

We had paid a UK based organisation to market our website, and it was doing very well in the search engine rankings. We were getting a huge amount of visits from people who were planning to move to the island and just wanted general advice. Although it was taking up more and more of our time, we were thoroughly enjoying helping people through a difficult planning process. During this time, we developed our relocation pack, which has been downloaded in big numbers on line ever since.

One question that cropped up regularly was "How do we secure a property to rent?" Initially we would send them a list of the few estate agents who dealt in rentals, but we were finding that there was a real shortage of long term rental property on Lanzarote. It was also interesting that I was seeing people walk into the estate agency on a daily basis asking about long term rental, and again we were sending those people off without any good news.

Having identified an opportunity in the market, Julie and I decided to see how we could develop it for Estupendo. Research showed us that the biggest problem was that most of the decent property on the island was being rented on holiday lets. Now holiday letting is much more lucrative than long term letting for owners, assuming they are getting a high occupancy rate. The big drawback from an owner's point of view is that there is cleaning and maintenance to organise, and generally there is much more wear and tear when a property is a holiday let, rather than used as someone's home. We started to approach some of the people we knew, to test our argument that long term letting was much more consistent, and a good deal less hassle – there was a mixed reaction, but one message that came across was that owners wouldn't pay us to rent their properties. In discussion with Spanish friends, we found that the norm here (and in most of

62

Europe) was that the tenants paid the agent's commission, and when we put that point to people, they seemed much more amenable to trying out long term rental.

The time had come to put our idea to the test, and we ran an advert in The Holiday Gazette. It ran something like this:

Property Owners!
Bored of holiday lets?
Tired of cleaning and maintenance bills?
Why not long term let your property?
No charges to you!
Call Estupendo etc etc.

The response wasn't staggering, but we had a few cautious calls, and met with some people who were potentially interested, and we visited their properties, agreed a rental price and took photos so that we could show our clients. We then had to develop a plan to ensure that we offered value for money to our tenants, as they were effectively paying for our service. We decided that we would continue to offer as much free help and advice as we could via e-mail and on the telephone, whilst at the same time offering them our rental properties when they expressed an interest. To this day, I still feel we "go the extra mile" with our clients – we'll collect them from the airport, or their previous home, we'll help them open bank accounts, get the children sorted in school, arrange the rental contracts, and be on hand for whatever help they need.

We found very quickly that getting tenants wasn't difficult – we had found a huge niche – but getting good properties was and still is a constant battle. Our first tenants were Vicky and Leo – a young couple who were planning a full time move to the island, and wanted a small apartment on a complex with a pool. Everything was done via e-mail, with us sending photos and details, and them sending a deposit by international transfer. I remember how nervous we were designing all the reservation and contract paperwork, and ensuring that the apartment was clean and ready for them. It seemed very odd at the time, to rent a property to someone who hadn't even seen it, but around a third of the rentals we do every month follow this pattern, and we have become used to describing properties very accurately, and, fortunately, we haven't disappointed anyone yet. Vicky and

63

Leo have since moved on twice (with Estupendo) and remain settled on the island.

It was an amazing feeling to have found a property, found some tenants and successfully seen the whole thing through to a conclusion. But already we had more people contacting us to find them properties, and so began a fairly manic period in our working lives where we seemed to spend every spare hour (outside of our full time jobs) trying to persuade owners to offer their places for long term rental, and then sorting the paperwork and getting the tenants installed.

As Estupendo was now making a decent income, it was time to formalise the company, and we went through the process of setting up the organisation in Spain, obtaining all the correct licences, and arranging to pay our taxes. This was long winded, but reasonably straightforward, with the help of an assessoria, a kind of government approved accountant.

I began to think how I could extricate myself from the estate agency, as I truly believed that given some real effort, Estupendo could now support me full time. Julie was more cautious, and was reluctant for me to give up the security of a contract, expenses and a basic salary.

Earlier in the year I had been approached by a friend, Keith, who was the advertising salesman for Power FM – he had asked if I would help with the broadcast of Ironman, which is the annual triathlon event held here, and which is renowned as the toughest in the world. Power was started 9 years previously by Gavin Watson, and his first transmissions were from his bedroom to a very small audience in Los Gigantes, Tenerife. Power is now the biggest broadcaster in The Canaries, covering all seven islands, and with offices in many of them. Gavin's a genuinely nice guy, and simply loves radio and all the technical stuff that goes with it. Ironman was to be their most ambitious project to date, bringing a full outside broadcast unit to Lanzarote, with radio mikes and so on. In order to fund the trip, they arranged a series of road shows across the island in the lead up the actual event. Being fascinated by radio myself, I offered Keith any support he needed. I helped to "Sell" a couple of the road shows, and he then asked me if I would record some interviews with contestants to be played on the day itself. So, armed with a mini disc player,

64

a very big microphone, and press passes, Julie and I attended the pre race press conference. I have to say this was a pretty scary experience – despite having worked for the newspaper, I still didn't really consider myself a journalist, and we were surrounded by people with "Daily Telegraph" and stuff like that on their badges. There were TV cameras everywhere, and most of the elite athletes seemed to know all the real journos. In the event we didn't say a word at the press conference, but wandered outside and got some quite good interviews with local athletes. Julie then spotted Bella Cummerford, the Scottish professional who had a good chance of wining the women's event, and I boldly walked up to her, and we had a half decent chat. She turned out to be a delightful lady, who was obviously much better at being interviewed than I was at doing the interviewing! The result was great, but the credit should all be hers. The Power team adopted her as "our" runner, and we cheered here every time she came past the unit during the race, and I even got a high five from her as she finished third on the day. She went on to win the event four years later.

On race morning, we arrived at the OBU at 6AM for the 7AM start. Now, I was expecting to be a gofer for the day, and Julie had come down to watch. Almost as soon as we arrived, Gavin was setting me up with a radio mike, and it gradually dawned on me that I was going to be commentating! Julie was immediately co-opted to sort out all the timing, and we were thrust into the fray! My commentating partner was the sports presenter from Power, Paul Webb, known to all as "Webby." He has since moved to Lanzarote and does his sports show from this island every Saturday, and remains a good friend. Webby is the fastest talking, most enthusiastic man you could ever meet, and I suspect that Gavin had realised that the combination of Webby's and my more measured "posher" speech would be a good one on air. He proved to be right and Webby and I have worked together many times since, and we do seem to have good radio chemistry. But back to race day – I hadn't even had time to dwell on the fact that we were broadcasting to the whole of The Canaries and the entire world over the internet, when Gavin counted us in for the lead up to the start. Even now, it makes my hair stand on end to remember the moment, and you will have seen the photo Julie took at the start of this chapter– it shows Webby and I, mikes in hand, with the sun coming up in Puerto del Carmen, and the swimmers about to enter the water. I hadn't had time to plan my

65

first words live on air, but they tumbled out anyway "Good Morning Webby, Good morning world! You're listening to Power FM live, and we're going to share the world's toughest sporting event with you. Welcome to Ironman 2003, coming to you from Puerto del Carmen in Lanzarote!" It was a fantastic day – the sporting action was memorable, Webby and I interviewed athletes, their families and spectators, Julie provided us with a constant stream of facts and figures we could talk about, and we really helped to establish Power as a force on the island, and their link with Ironman remains a strong one. The broadcast ran from 7AM until we handed back to the studio at 9PM, by which time all the serious athletes had long finished. It had been a long and exciting day, but as we were heading back, there were around 60 competitors still running the marathon leg up and down passed our OBU. We were all ecstatic, but emotionally and physically drained and headed to the bars for a few well earned beers.

Months later, when we were in the difficult phase of trying to get me into Estupendo full-time, Keith (the Power Salesman) asked me if I would consider working with him to sell the advertising. The agreement he had was that he was effectively a franchisee, running his own business as a subcontractor to Power, and keeping a percentage of the income. I looked at his business, which was providing a steady, but fairly low income, and compared it to ours, which was stronger overall, but very inconsistent. It occurred to me that we could combine the two businesses, with Power providing a baseline and Estupendo providing "The Cream." We spent many hours with Keith and his partner, working on business plans, and then we were offered incredibly cheap office space in Playa Honda by some friends. I was convinced that spending more time working on Estupendo, and adding some sales and marketing flare to selling advertising, would result in both businesses working even better than previously. We made the decision to go for it, and I handed my notice in at the estate agency.

We duly visited the assessor to set up the new partnership, bought some second hand office furniture, and Josh and I decorated the office. I remember arriving for my first day full of enthusiasm, having no idea that I'd just made a massive mistake!

66

The partnership lasted two months. Estupendo took off in a big way – it seemed that as soon as I put effort into Estupendo, it reaped rewards in terms of income from renters. Whilst the same was true with Power, the profit was much lower. I was in a position where I needed income to support the family, and I could see that every day I spent working on Estupendo, I was achieving what we needed, but with the advertising sales, I was getting about half of what was required. Another problem I faced was that Keith really didn't want to know about Estupendo. Despite the fact that it was paying more than half of his salary, he very much considered it to be "My thing", whilst he focussed almost solely on the radio sales. We also had some serious issues in terms of working style, and I was becoming increasingly concerned. The upside was that I now knew that Estupendo could support us, so I took the only decision I could and ended the partnership. I moved out of the office and into our spare bedroom and focussed my energies solely on our own venture. It was a difficult time, and our friendship with Keith and his partner has never been repaired – he subsequently lost his franchise with Power a year or so later and was replaced by a new marketing team. I have remained good friends with Gavin and the guys and girls at the station, and continue to work with them from time to time.

We were now well and truly on our own – with only one fixed wage, and running the business from home again. It was scary stuff at the time, but Estupendo did us proud, and from that moment to this we have enjoyed real success with the business.

Chapter 13 – Heading North!

As the business began to get stronger, we started to think about where we were living. We loved Arrecife, and we loved our apartment, but we had taken it at a time when we had needed to reduce our outgoings, and there were three major drawbacks for us. One, we missed having decent outdoor space, two it wasn't in the best area of Arrecife and three our Landlord downstairs was proving to be a bit of a problem. It seemed he was a real drinker, and I don't think his wife was too impressed when he was on the bottle. This resulted in some huge rows, which seemed to go on for hours and at very high volume.

I had a bizarre experience with him one day. Underneath the apartment was a garage, accessed by the narrowest, steepest driveway you can imagine. The landlord knocked on the door one day, and told me that his car (a Renault Twingo) was stuck in the garage with a flat battery. He asked if we could use my car to jump start it. Now My Fiat wasn't exactly huge, but I had to fold the mirrors in to squeeze down the driveway, and once down in the garage, there wasn't much room to move. We connected up the batteries, and he proceeded to churn his starter motor in 30 second bursts. I quickly realised that the problem with the Renault was more than just a battery one, and I persuaded him to let me take a plug out to see if there was a spark. I showed him that there wasn't, and explained that he needed someone to check the electrics out. He still insisted that it would start and proceeded to run the start motor until the jump leads were almost melting. At that point I stopped him, and told him again to call a mechanic. We removed the jump leads, and I looked at the drive, wondering how I was going to get back out in reverse. He must have read my mind, because he told me that there was no way to do that – he told me that we would have to turn the car around first. Before I could react, he had jumped in and proceeded to carry out a 12 point turn in the very confined space. I began to relax, as despite the smell of alcohol on his breath, he seemed to be judging each point well. That was until the last two points, where he damaged the front, and then the back bumper. I was cringing as he finally got the car pointing the right way. I prepared myself to get back in, but he was now on a roll, and decided to drive the car right out for me. He gave it about 4000RPM, and then crawled up the hill with a huge amount of clutch slip. By the time he reached the top (it seemed to take about 10 minutes to me) there were clouds of smoke coming from the engine and the smell of fried clutch was choking me. He paused at the top on enough to apply full lock and then put the handbrake on and jumped out. He walked passed me without a word of apology or thanks, and so I stomped up the drive to get my damaged pride and joy back safely onto the road. Jumping in, I decided to save the clutch any more pain, and dropped it quickly, forgetting he had already applied lots of steering – I could have cried as I heard the rear wing scrape against the wall. I parked the car, hoping the clutch would recover, but it didn't. That little episode cost me several hundred euros for the new clutch and the paintjob, and the landlord never even acknowledged his contribution. It was another reason to move on.

In family discussions, we decided that we wanted to stay in Arrecife, and we had watched the construction of a new apartment block near us with interest. Calling into the relevant estate agents in town one day, we checked out the price and plans, and took everything home to show the kids. All of us agreed on a particular apartment, and we duly put a deposit on our new place, which would take several more months to be completed. We were going to be home owners again! It was fun watching the construction, and planning our furniture, things couldn't happen fast enough for us.

When we were about three months away from completion, I had reason to go out to Punta Mujeres one day, and I took a moment to revisit the small community of houses I had taken on for the estate agency to sell. Last time I had been there, the site had been all concrete blocks, but now they were almost completed. I immediately fell in love with the place. Natural materials had been used all around, with volcanic rock walls, stone flooring, wooden decking, a wooden bridge and swimming pool. The six houses were just 50 Meters from the sea, and the village had a couple of little bars, a restaurant and a bakery in it. I fantasised about living there, and imagined one day using the little slipway at the bottom of the road to launch our own boat. I even took Julie out to see the houses, but the price was way out of our reach, and we soon forgot about them.

69

Then fate dealt a hand, and the developers contacted us to say they were retaining two for long term rental, and asked Estupendo to take them on. We immediately negotiated to take one on rental, and they even agreed to an option to buy, which we were to take up a year later. We managed to get our original deposit on the new apartment back, and set about planning our move up north.

We had rented unfurnished and had a great time buying all our furniture and fixings. We were charmed about the way the small furniture shops in Arrecife took everything on trust. No need for a deposit, no need to pay for delivery, just pay the driver for the goods when he gets there!

We had committed ourselves to the move when we had a call from the builders to tell us that the electricity and water hadn't been connected, but they would make a "temporary" arrangement. Water wasn't a problem as all houses in Lanzarote are built with aljibes, or wells, as the water supply is pretty erratic. We knew that we could run on the aljibe for at least a couple of weeks, and that it would simply be a case of refilling ours from a neighbours hose. Electricity was a bigger problem, but the builders got around that by connecting our house (and the community lighting and pool supply) to a neighbours outlet. The problem, of course, was that this was too much for one circuit, and the neighbour in question lived in Arrecife during the week. As a result, whenever we managed to trip the supply, it necessitated calling him over and waiting at least an hour without electricity. We quickly became adept at turning off the pool pumps and community lighting whenever we wanted to cook! Our biggest problem was the two waterfalls in the swimming pool, which were on a timer and would come on at inopportune moments, leaving me screaming around the house turning things off! This temporary arrangement lasted for around three months, and to this day I hesitate when I turn the cooker on, half expecting to be plunged into darkness.

Teething troubles aside, we all loved our new home, and Tia revelled in the outside space, spending hours sleeping on the patio. We loved the proximity to the sea, which we could hear all the time, and we all spent hours enjoying the pool, the village and all the fantastic walks in the area.

70

The village is very quiet during the week, but comes alive at the weekend – many of the houses are owned by people who live in Arrecife, and they use them as weekend homes. They arrive on a Friday night, open garages to reveal jet skis, quads and speedboats, and spend all weekend playing! We had one local copper, one local taxi driver and a small sociedad which had a football and boules pitch. The people were fantastic and it was a real pleasure to be part of the small community.

We had plenty of other trying times, which we now know are common on new build here, and which are worth recounting in this story. I began to get a bit worried when the water in our aljibe started to become very cloudy. It seems the wrong paint had been used, and it was leeching into the water supply. The builders decided to call in experts, who suggested relining them with pool lining material. We went off to work and school one morning, having been told that the plumbers were coming in. They spent the day draining and drying our aljibe and promptly knocked off, leaving us without water! This went on for three days, with us filling the toilet cisterns from the swimming pool. Eventually they had us reconnected, and all was well for a few days when suddenly our supply stopped again. They couldn't get anybody out to us on the day (inevitably a Sunday) so Josh and I set about trying to get things going again. We managed to work out how the system here works (basically an electric pump with non return valves) and established where the problem was. The hard bit was getting water back into the pipe work, which had become filled with air. I had to stand on tiptoe, pouring water out of a 5 litre container, into a small round pipe above my head. It took about twelve attempts, and I was left thoroughly soaked, but was eventually triumphant. The other nightmare was the first time it rained. The skylight leaked, the drain at the back blocked, and our bedroom balcony turned out to slope into rather than away from our house. The result was that we had water pouring into all three floors of the house. We subsequently sorted the first two problems, but the balcony continued to leak, and we ended up with a temporary pipe which we put up there when it rained – fortunately not something that happens too often here!

None of these things took the shine away, and they are so typically Spanish that it would almost have been disappointing not to have endured some of them. This part of the island suits us well, and I didn't ever expect to move far.

71

Chapter Fourteen – Friends and Family

When we lived in UK, we were ten minutes walk from Julie's mum's house, and yet in the years we have been here, more than two thousand miles away, I have got to know her far better than I ever did during our snatched moments over Sunday lunch. And the same applies to the rest of the family, most of whom have been to Lanzarote, and many of whom have stayed with us. Julie's mum Jenny and her partner Norman have been here many times, have bought property here, and are in the process of planning a permanent move. Those of you who can remember back as far as the first chapter of this book will know that it was Jenny who introduced us to the island, and we in turn have helped to persuade her and Norman that their future lies here with us. Julie's brother and sister, together with their families have all enjoyed Lanzarote, and we have spent many joyful hours with our nephews.

The children I shared with my first wife, who are now both grown up, have been to visit and enthused at our new style of life. I cannot overemphasise the benefit of giving our families time, and getting to know them so much better than we ever did in our busy UK style lives.

Many of the best laughs along the way have come from friends who have stayed with us. Our closest friends in UK were Chris and Sharon, and they have been our most frequent visitors having stayed at all three of our homes. Now Chris is a mad keen fisherman, and each time he visits he brings more and more gear with him – he even buys extra stuff when he's out here! My garage is bursting at the seams with some pretty impressive tackle, about seven rods, and dozens of reels. Unfortunately, Chris is either not a very good fisherman, or maybe he's just very unlucky! He will often head out as I'm leaving for work and return late evening, tanned and healthy looking, and almost always fishless! After the first couple of visits, we decided to get him a special present, and in collusion with Sharon, we hired a deep sea fishing boat for the day. As we arrived at Puerto Calero, and met the skipper, he pointed out the huge starboard rod on the boat, which was bent about 20 degrees. He told us that the marlin were running and that they had caught a record fish the previous day. Chris was almost shaking with excitement at the prospect of wrestling a 200 kilo beast aboard, and we set off for the channel between Lanzarote and Fuerteventura. What none of us (including Chris) had realised is that he has a tendency to sea sickness and within half an hour, he had gone an interesting green colour! He managed to fight through his discomfort, and while the rest of us enjoyed lying on deck in the sunshine, Chris paced the stern waiting for the big bite. Inevitably, with him aboard, there wasn't a single nibble all day, and we returned to port without so much as a sprat, and promptly enjoyed a marvellous fish meal in a local restaurant.

It was around this time that I started to take the mickey out of Chris for his lack of success, and he redoubled his efforts to provide us with something we could cook on the barbecue. The first time he caught a decent fish was in Puerto del Carmen one hot and very sunny day. The rest of us had been snorkelling and he managed to land a fair sized, if ugly thing. After proudly displaying it, we all agreed it was time to celebrate with a beer. Chris put the fish into a fair sized rock pool, and we climbed up the rocks to the nearest bar to watch the sun set and to contemplate the fabulous meal we would have when we got home. We watched various people stop to admire the fish swimming in the rock pool below us and I could see Chris brimming with pride. A lone lady appeared and she too stopped to have a good look. Before we had time to react, she reached into the pool, grabbed the fish and hurled it into the sea! The rest of us burst out laughing, but Chris leapt down to the beach and asked the lady what she thought she was doing. "Well, I thought it was stuck in the rock pool, so I threw it into the sea!"

On another occasion, Chris did come home with a decent fish, which we all thoroughly enjoyed, although he was strangely quiet throughout the meal. After several glasses of wine he burst forth with "I can't lie any longer – I swapped it with another fisherman for some tackle!"

On another trip, shortly after we had bought a speedboat, Chris had wanted to fish from the boat, but the sea had been very rough all week. This visit coincided with that of some other very good friends, Peter and Linda. Both Peter and Chris had been badgering me all week to take them out on the boat, and on their last day the wind was still blowing and there were 2 meter waves. I told them both that I was happy to go out – I'm blessed

73

with very good sea legs – but that it might be uncomfortable for them. But they were determined and so we set off from the little harbour. As soon as we hit open sea we were leaping all over the place, and the boys got very wet. I found a nice reef to anchor off and settled back in my seat as they prepared their tackle. Now just about the worst thing you can do in a small boat that's bobbing up and down is concentrate on a detailed task, and within minutes they were both looking queasy. After regular stops, staring grimly at the horizon, they finally got their lines into the water. Within about thirty seconds Chris threw up over the side, which caused Peter great amusement and to crack "That'll bring the fish out!" Peter lasted at least 5 minutes before he too, lost his lunch, and we headed back to port with me grinning my head off and the two boys consoling each other and thinking about the large medicinal brandies they were about to consume.

As well as visiting friends, we now have a huge network of friends on the island. Lanzarote is an incredibly democratic place, and status and money aren't relevant when it comes to getting to know people, and our new friends come from all walks of life. We were introduced to Wendy and Alan Lambert by some other people, and we have become great mates with them. They're interesting, well travelled and great fun. They live at Charco del Palo, which is the naturist village a couple of kilometres from us. Wendy and Alan have been naturists for years, and Charco is a fabulous place for them as the whole village is basically a nude area. Over the years, I have had a standing joke with them – whenever we're on our way down to them, I call and tell them to get their kit on! Love them though we do, we had no intention of taking our own clothes off, or of seeing them naked. Until the day they invited us for a meal with two other friends. Now I didn't bother calling, as they knew what time we were expected. So we parked the car and strolled around to the back patio, with me shouting my standard "Get your kit on, Mike and Julie are here!" I heard a muffled "Oh sh*t!" as I rounded the corner to find all four of them starkers! Nobody had been watching the time, and they were caught out by our arrival. It was too late to do anything, so we just carried on and had a few beers, and they all dressed for dinner.

Another couple who have become lifelong mates are Brian and Beverly Barrell. Although they still live in UK and run their

74

business there, they have a house in our village and come out at least six times a year. We really look forward to their visits and always have a fabulous time with them, and it was Brian who got me into scuba diving, for which I will remain grateful until my last breath.

Brian has been diving for twenty or so years and is both a very good and a very experienced diver. He had been diving with a German dive school based in Costa Teguise for many years, and when I expressed an interest in trying it, he arranged for me to do a try dive with them. The school was owned and run by Monika and Christian, who became good friends, and to whom I recommended any interested divers. It was Monika who originally trained me, and continued to do so as I worked my way up to instructor level. She is classically German, very direct and forthright. One has to be careful not to make passing comments to her, as she takes everything literally. An example was an early conversation when I said that she and Christian should come round for a barbecue "some time." Her immediate response was (insert your own German accent at this point):
"When?"
"Erm, Saturday?"
"At what time?"
"Erm, eight?"
"Good, you will buy and prepare the fish, and I will buy and prepare the salad and bread, see you on Saturday."

I'm very fortunate in that the dive school was right near my office, so I have always been able to dive a lot, in fact I do more dives in a year than most UK divers manage in ten. My most regular partner is Brian, and he and I have shared some memorable experiences, enjoying angel sharks, huge rays, enormous grouper and some fantastic cave dives.

One particularly funny experience was the time we dived a wreck in Arrecife harbour. Now Brian is a great collector when he's diving and regularly brings up stuff from the sea bed, and I gather his house in UK is a treasure trove of cannon balls and the like. On this particular dive we had been deep for some time, and we had been amazed at how intact the wreck was. Brian had found a huge brass porthole and tried to open it. We were both surprised when it came away in his hands! I could tell from his face that he really wanted this porthole for his collection, but we

75

didn't have any lifting bags, so I could see him thinking about finding a way to secure it for another visit with bags. At this point our air supply was quite low, but if we just left it on the sea bed it would soon be covered in silt. Brian started pointing up to the buoy which marked the wreck, and it dawned on me that he wanted to secure the porthole to it. At this point we were at around 30 meters depth and the buoy was some 60 meters (the length of the vessel) away from us. We both grabbed the porthole and by gently inflating our jackets we managed to manhandle it onto the deck if the ship. Once there, we bounded along the deck, like men on the moon, and got to below the buoy. This was going to be the really tricky bit – controlling our ascent with this massive weight. We got onto the buoy's rope and with little puffs of air, we made it to within 5 meters of the surface. At that point, and dangerously low on air, we decided to tie the porthole onto the buoy – far enough down that other plunderers wouldn't see it! This was a really tricky thing to do – we had to control our own buoyancy, whilst being prepared to dump air as soon as we let go, as bursting up to the surface is extremely dangerous, even life threatening. At the same time as thinking about this, we were desperately tying loads of knots in the rope to the porthole, and watching our air gauges go into the red. Having put enough knots in the rope, we looked at each other wide eyed, both understanding that we had to get our timing absolutely right. We each held the porthole in our right hands and our air dump valves in the left. I nodded my head once, twice and on the third we dumped all our air and let go of our massive burden. I looked first to make sure I wasn't ascending and about to burst a lung, and as soon as I realised I had remained at five meters I looked forward to make sure the knots had held. I was totally confused to see the rope, and no porthole, and then it dawned on me that the rope was moving..............fast! I looked down to see the porthole heading for the bottom, and then looked up to see to buoy coming straight down at me! I looked at Brian and saw recognition dawn on him and we both swam out of the way just in time for the buoy to come between us. The porthole hit the sea bed in a cloud of silt, and the buoy settled a perfect five meters above it – and twenty five meters below the surface. Brian looked at me, removed his regulator and mouthed a single word – one that begins with "F".

With no air left we had to make straight for the surface to find that we were several hundred meters from the boat, and in the swell, it was unlikely that the boys aboard would see us. Brian said "Nothing else for it, Mike, snorkels in and a long swim." I inflated my jacket with my last drop of air and got my head down. It was exhausting, but I kept going until I got to the boat, and looked round to see how far behind Brian was. He was nowhere to be seen! I clambered aboard, and urged to guys to get the motor going, keeping one eye on our previous bearing. We motored the distance in no time at all, and half way there I spotted Brian lying calmly in the water floating on his jacket. Fuming, I shouted "What happened?"

"No point in both of us swimming all that way" Came back the logical reply. As I said at the beginning, a very experienced diver! We rescued the buoy the following day, but it took us four years to find our porthole!

As the business has expanded, our social life has moved along with it, as we often become good friends with our clients once they're on the island. Weekends these days are about limiting the numbers at our house or deciding which of several invitations we can actually take up!

Chapter Fifteen – Estupendo's First Office

At this time, we were still running Estupendo from home, although the set up was a bit more sophisticated than one might imagine. One of our biggest frustrations was that we couldn't get broadband in our village in those days, so although our network of two PC's was pretty sophisticated, our connection to the outside world was pretty slow. There was also the problem that our home had become a hang out through the summer months for many local kids, mainly because we had one of the few swimming pools in the area. So despite the fact that the office was in the basement, we were regularly disturbed by what sounded like galloping herds of rampant elephants, accompanied by large troops of cackling monkeys. The final difficulty was one faced by many people who work from home – a classic double edged sword. Whilst it was a pleasure to be able to relax and take a break in the comfort of my own home, there was also always the temptation to "just check email" on a Sunday morning – which almost inevitably turned into a three hour work session. Strangely enough, working from home often means actually working many more hours, and I now thoroughly enjoy the journey home, gradually switching off and knowing that I can't actually do anything but enjoy life until I unlock the office door again.

With this in mind, Julie and I had been putting feelers out for office space. As she was still working part time elsewhere, and I needed to be out and about a good deal, we needed somewhere ideally with some other cover for the phones. The offer of a place in Youths United's offices came at just the right moment for us. We knew and liked the other people in there, and they would be around to handle enquiries and answer the phone when we weren't. We agreed a very acceptable portion of the rent, and also had the use of their more sophisticated office machinery.

Julie and I spent a very enjoyable weekend installing our network, desks and telephones and had a fabulous Eureka moment when we once again connected to the internet on a broadband connection. Estupendo had arrived in the 21st century! We designed a sign and had it made by our signwriter, Phil Wright. and proudly displayed the Estupendo logo on the roof. Phil is an interesting character – he is a truly old fashioned sign writer, able to draw the most amazing designs freehand. He has become a valued supplier over the years, helping us with a good deal of our design and helping to promote our business in many ways. He produced the Estupendo decals we have on the doors of our cars, as well as recreating Manrique's Lanzarote Sun symbol in silver on our van – it looks stunning, seeming to come out of the bodywork, and makes the van instantly recognisable anywhere on the island.

The office itself was pretty small, and our space within it was less than 20 square meters – basically two desks and half of a large window to display our properties. But the location was splendid! Only 100 meters from the sea, with fabulous views and next door to a cracking snack and sandwich bar called Smiley's and owned by a good friend Gemma. The décor was a little strange, with purple walls and a peculiar serpent-like light unit dominating the ceiling, but we did install a comfortable couch for our clients – something that was to become a feature of all our premises once we had outgrown the original.

What we hadn't realised was how much of an impact having a premises would have, and the number of rentals we were doing increased rapidly, especially with Julie now spending more and more time in the business. Estupendo had grown into a well recognised brand on the island by this time, and I was surprised to hear us described as the largest rental agency on the island by an estate agent, but thinking about it I realised he was right.

Julie's impact on the business was phenomenal, and out of all proportion to the part time hours she was working. She is a fantastic relationship builder, and has turned many clients into life long friends simply through being herself. She is also the perfect administrator, and is well organised, always in control of the finances and is blessed with an amazing memory. I think many people have the impression that Estupendo is my company, as I'm the talker and "front man", but the reality is that I merely steer the ship and try to plot our future course. All of the motive power is provided by Julie, and I am happy to admit that in every area bar actually selling to clients, she is far more competent than me. There is an old saying that married couples shouldn't work together – well I dispute that wholeheartedly, as long as your skills are complimentary, it can work incredibly well.

79

Those first few months were amazing – I really enjoyed coming into the office every day and it turned out to be an incredible summer here, with temperatures in the forties. It was impossible to wear anything resembling business clothing, so we adopted smart shorts and surf wear, a tradition we have continued and which sets us apart from the other agents on the island. Coming in with the sun rising over the sea, then taking a break to walk along the beach at lunchtime, followed by a swift drink on the way home – this really was the life.

As a result of the increase in business, we started to struggle towards the end of the summer, being unable to cope with the amount of work we were generating. This left us on the horns of a dilemma. Although we were earning good money, we were working too hard! The sensible thing would be for Julie to leave her part time (but very well paid) job at the hotel, but she was reluctant to give up the guaranteed security that the mortgage and bills would be covered whatever Estupendo did. We were in the classic dilemma all small businesses face – expand or stay small and keep it simple. The other thing that was affecting our decision was that we had for some time been thinking we should be offering houses for sale as well as rental – particularly because so many of our rental clients were buying property a few months after arriving. We figured that as we already had a good relationship with them, that they would be happy to consider us when looking to buy, and so it has proved. But this would require yet more administrative support for me.

Help arrived in the shape of Tila and Michelle, with whom we had been sharing our office for some time. They had spent many years building, buying and renting property on the island and had themselves toyed with the idea of starting an estate agency, rather than continually paying other people to help them buy and sell property. We agreed to sell them shares in Estupeno, and we all agreed to expand the business and to start selling properties as well.

Our first step was to set a formal company up, as we had until that point been trading with me simply as a self employed person. Estupendo CB was born, and had a licence to trade as a rental and sales company and we were off and running!

80

Things quickly settled into our new office and routine, and we really enjoyed working together and spending time next door at Smileys enjoying their super food and coffee. It was a lovely environment, with the beach a hundred meters away and spending time with windsurfing chums.

Michelle became adept at supporting Julie on the administration side and we made our first few sales in what seemed like no time at all.

This was a period of rapid expansion, as we were generating good income and using that to great benefit by upgrading our marketing and website. During this time I had been contacted by Nick Bird, who had started emailing me about our website more than a year previously. Each time we spoke, he asked me if he could make an appointment to talk about how he could improve our website, and each time I put him off as we didn't really want to spend more money on it. However, the time had come when we could, and I finally agreed to see him.

Nick arrived in the office looking anything but a computer techie! He's tall and slim, habitually wears a white sleeveless vest and sports a crucifux earring in one ear. I also learned he hosts Karaoke and quiz nights in various bars as a hobby! I was a bit dubious at first, but he seemed to ask a lot of questions about our business, and then agreed to go away to think about it, before producing a proposal. When the document arrived a week later I was stunned! Not only had he produced a really professional report, but he had also really "got under the skin" of Estupendo, and understood our needs perfectly. He proposed a radical revamp of our entire network and systems, as well as a complete redesign of the website. The bad news was that there was no way we could afford it all, and I told him so. He then represented the document, suggesting the various stages we could go through, with their attached costs. I'm happy to say we followed his advice and Nick became almost a part of our business, knowing how we work, and always suggesting new methods of improving our services. We eventually completed all the work he originally suggested, and the result was that we had something I was extremely proud of, and probably the most advanced computer system in any estate agency on the island. The level of sophistication was up to the standard of major corporations I had worked with in the past, using SQL servers and administering

81

our own email and web network. We had two completely independent broadband networks, one with wireless, and some amazing internal web processes that mean we could input details and photos once, and the system could build webpages and a variety of reports for us from that single input. The website, as a consequence was constantly updated – I could return from valuing a property and it could be up on the website within 20 minutes! We could also access our full system from any computer anywhere in the world. Anyway, enough of the nerdy stuff – it was pretty damn good for its time!

The biggest spin off of having the new office was that we suddenly seemed to have people visiting us all the time – and not just people who were looking for property, but also existing customers dropping in for a chat, some advice or just to network with other people. We'd sort of become a drop in centre, and this was eventually to lead us to design Esinfo in the future.

During this period, one set of customers that stands out in my mind were Tony and Louise Doyle. I had been in touch with Louise for several months on email. The couple had decided they wanted to live in Lanzarote, but had planned a month here to make sure it was the right decision. They had already become long term subscribers to our newsletter, had purchased our relocation pack, and had booked the full day island tour during their trip. They had arranged their own accommodation for the months "trial", but I had agreed to meet them at the airport and take them there on the first day. After getting lost in the dark of Guime, we finally found their place, and I agreed to collect them the next day for the island tour. I really enjoy these tours – I'm extremely proud of Lanzarote and simply love showing the island and its beauty to people – it's a real pleasure watching their faces as they see the island through my eyes. I can honestly say that this place still takes my breath away at least once week, and no matter how hard things have been, I never hesitate to thank my lucky stars that I chose this as my home.

Anyway, back to Tony and Louise – we really hit it off on that trip around the island. They're good people – honest, hard working and good company, and I sensed that we would become friends in the future. We had a "spare" car at the time – Julie's old Seat Marbella, which we had christened "Bella", and we agreed to lend them the car for the rest of the trip, so they didn't

82

use too much budget hiring one. Off they went on the following day, and I seemed to see them out and about everywhere over the next few weeks. We did have a laugh one day, when Louise called Julie to tell her that the Gear lever had come off in her hand in the middle of Puerto del Carmen! What could have been a nightmare was easily resolved with a quick call to The British Garage in PDC, who sent a guy out who fixed the problem in no time at all. This was the start of a series of car problems which Tony and Louise seemed to permanently suffer from.

They were still on the island at the time we were planning Julie's birthday party and we invited them along. They met a lot of our friends at that event, and became part of our wide circle of mates on the island. The party was great! Marina Rubicon in Playa Blanca had just opened and we had heard about their fabulous full moon parties at Café del Mar. We booked into a great hotel and really enjoyed the atmosphere, with fire eaters, exotic dancers and good music – a great night was had by all.

After their month, they finally decided to make the break and they found a tenant for their place in UK, and booked to move into an apartment we had on our books in Arrieta. Once they had arrived, we helped Tony get work as a painter and decorator and we found Louise a job at a big hotel complex in Costa Teguise. We had two new customers, but much more importantly, we had two new friends, and ultimately we ended up working with them both. Almost as soon as Louise started at the hotel, we'd decided we needed some more administration support. We mentioned this to her and she quit her job to join us.

Where once there was just little old me, we were suddenly many! With Julie, Louise and myself full time and Michelle part-time, I really had to adjust my way of working. Where I had got used to knowing every aspect of the business, and more importantly every customer, I now was finding more and more that I was only part of the team. This took some getting used to, and my mental and physical filing systems came in for some serious stick from my colleagues.

As has always happened when we have taken on more people, we found there was an immediate positive impact on the business, with rentals flying in thick and fast, and sales doing well too. We were already cramped in our little shared office and

83

our thoughts began to turn to finding more space. At the same time we were approached by a friend, Huseyin, who wanted to come and work with us. Huseyin joined us initially on a part time basis, but bea¡came a fully fledged member of staff, having proved himself adept at doing business with island locals, an area where we had always been weak.

Settled into the little office on the sea front, we really began to make an impact on the local market and were soon renting and selling properties all over the island.

Chapter Sixteen – Buying a Complete Ruin

During this time, Julie's Mum had visited us, and she was interested in buying another property over here, but she was looking for somewhere to "do up" in the north of the island. Tila contacted one of his friends who told us about a large ruin in Haría, which was available, and we arranged to go up there with her to see it.

The day is firmly etched in my mind, as it was the start of a long, long road which even today we are only a little along. It was raining quite heavily, and we pulled up in two cars. We knew that there was someone else on the point of putting an offer in, and also that the sale process would be complicated by the fact that the property was owned by something like eight children who had inherited it. As we pulled up, I peered through the gloom to see a huge house, covered in overgrown cactus and in a huge plot of land, right in the middle of Haría.

We got out, and we were introduced to Domingo, the head of the family who lived across the road. He started by telling us the story of the house. It had been built 135 years earlier, and had been a grand family home. The main house had 14 rooms and there was a separate "house" attached which had been the camel sheds at one time! There were three huge palm trees in the garden – one planted each for Domingo, his father and his grandfather. The house was set between two barrancos, and was the only house in the village with natural water wells, of which there were two. The last occupant had been Domingo's Dad, who had lived in two or three rooms while the rest fell down around him, but he had passed on ten years earlier.

We wandered around the place and found cactus and bougainvillea growing in some rooms, the remains of a smoke house and Canarian oven, and lovely features like intact troughs to feed the animals. The huge garden (almost an acre) was very overgrown with cactus and tumbleweed, but there was a whole row of grapevines which might be saved. I had a feeling of peace and tranquillity immediately, and that feeling remains today.

It was obvious that it would be a project of immense proportions and wasn't the type of thing Jenny was looking for, but we all
85

wandered around getting a very good feeling. The house was simply too big. Then Jenny hit on an idea – we could buy it together and work on it together. She and Norman would take the main house, and Julie, myself and the kids could convert the camel sheds into a fabulous three bedroom home with swimming pool.

It was immediately appealing – we could between us convert one wing of the main house into two guest suites, so our guests could stay there as well, and we would all have use of what could be an amazing garden.

We already knew the price, which was frankly a bargain, but we huddled and decided we would make an offer. Domingo took us across to his house and we all sat down in straight backed chairs. As soon as he heard the word "Offer", he explained that he already had a buyer lined up who was looking into the restoration, but if we wanted it and were prepared to "shake" on the day, he would sell to us at his full asking price. After very little hesitation, we agreed and shook his hand.

We shot up to the nearest open bar – Mesón La Frontera, which has since become a favourite - and celebrated with a glass of wine. Having persuaded the owner to stay open for us, I then promptly smashed a bottle of wine in my excitement, but despite this the owner, Freddy and his wife are firm friends today.

We went to bed that night, fuelled by red wine, talking grandly about creating a generational family home, but not realising that it would be seven long, hard months until we would finally walk into the finca as the new owners!

The first problem we faced was that there were simply so many people involved. There were eight people who owned the house through inheritance and they were spread across both Las Islas Canarias and the peninsular, and they couldn't agree on anything from how much deposit we should pay, to when we could actually complete the sale.

The next thing that arose was that the house had last legally changed hands (through inheritance again) back in 1938. The bright spark who inherited it had the size of the land under declared to save tax by about 50%. Understandably, we wanted

86

the full 3500 meters of land put onto the deeds, and this necessitated getting the town hall to come and measure it.

Halfway through this whole process, one of the owners tragically died, which meant his three children were now part of the process, bringing the total sellers up to 10!

We never did pay a deposit, or sign a purchase contract, as the sellers couldn't agree on how much or when. But we did finally get a call from our lawyer to tell us that all the parties were organised and we could attend the notary to pay for the property and sign the escritura.

After a pretty traumatic session at the notary in a room designed to cater for four people, we finally had the keys and went to revisit what would become our new home. The story of the start of the restoration project is a whole new chapter, and one we will revisit for many years to come, but more of that later!

Chapter Seventeen – Christmas Back in UK

We celebrated out very first Christmas on the island by visiting Arrieta beach, firing up a barbecue and cooking turkey kebabs, and then took great delight in calling all our friends and family and asking them to "Guess where we're calling from?"

There followed a few years where we decided to return to UK in order to spend Christmas with our loved ones. Looking back, I think we had a false expectation. In our minds Christmas was the ideal of crisp, clear mornings, a light dusting of snow and happy shopkeepers. The reality was somewhat different!

Our final trip was in December 2003, and shortly following this trip we made a family decision that we wouldn't return to UK anymore, save for business, weddings and funerals. Instead we would use our holidays to explore the Spanish mainland and the rest of Europe.

We flew off the island on Christmas Eve, and it was a novel experience as we were on Monarch's largest wide bodied aircraft, and there were about 30 of us aboard! The service was superb, and we had acres of space. We arrived in Manchester late in the evening and headed for Jenny and Norman's house where they put us up in fine style.

Christmas day was wonderful, and we all enjoyed the company of brothers, sisters and their kids, and we had the full traditional turkey and trimmings.

On Boxing Day we decided to take advantage of the sales and headed to The Trafford Centre. After four years in Lanzarote, it was terrifying! It occurred to me at one point that there were more people in that one shopping centre than the entire population of our island! Whilst we enjoyed and marvelled at the choice available in the shops, we really struggled to keep together and find the things we were looking for. A couple of things were particularly hard to cope with. We were used to shopping centres being open to the elements, but in UK they are almost hermetically sealed and seemed so stuffy to us. The other strange thing was that everyone was ignoring us. In Lanzarote, it's the custom for complete strangers to shout "Hola" as they walk past, or at the very least to make eye contact and nod. Here in Manchester it struck us that people had their heads and eyes down and there was no feeling of community at all.

After the shopping trip we headed out to some other retail places and only stopped buying when we thought our cases would be full. Then we headed off to visit our friends around Warrington. The welcome was amazing, and everyone seemed to feed us so much food that I'm sure we all put loads of weight on.

Our next stop was Dorset, where we went to visit my family, and the weather turned very, very cold just in time for us to join my daughter Natalie in her unheated cottage. It was a beautiful place, but right out in the country and the only heating was via a log fire. Having spent a few years acclimatising to Lanzarote, we all really struggled to stay warm enough, but it was great to see our Dorset family on their home turf, and we enjoyed some really good pub lunches and dinners with them. By this time we were all suffering with colds and feeling a little grotty.

Driving was difficult – not just coping with right hand drive, but also dealing with the speed and aggression of UK motorists. We spend most of our time here pootling around at 90KPH, which is around 55 Miles per hour, so 80, 90 or 100 seems very fast and one really has to concentrate. Lanzaroteño drivers are pretty poor, but because of that allowances are made. If someone pulls out in front of you, you simply brake and don't worry about it, in UK people were very quick onto their horns whenever we hesitated for a moment.

Next we headed for Sussex to enjoy an elaborately planned joke. I have referred to Brian and Bev in previous chapters. They live in Sussex but have a home here on the island and over the years we have become very close. Ever since I'd known him, Brian had been going on about how wonderful his local pub, The Plough in Plumpton Green, was. I had always wanted to visit him there and we had contacted Bev and their daughters Katie and Wendy to let them know we would be in Plumpton on the Sunday lunchtime. All they had to do was get Brian to the pub, which was never going to be a difficult task. Bev had kindly offered to put us up, so she prepared the guest rooms without Brian's knowledge.

89

Everything was coordinated beautifully on the day – Brian's family were outside and he was in the bar ordering the drinks when I walked in. He did the most classic double take. You could almost hear the cogs turning as he tried to deal with seeing his Lanzarote friends in the local! We had plenty of drinks and then returned to their house for a fabulous meal. At one point Brian asked me where we were staying, and I really enjoyed saying "Your place!"

The following day we carried on east to Canterbury and Margate. My intention was to show Julie and the kids my old school, as we had a day to kill before returning to London, and then home.

We all enjoyed the tour of Canterbury Cathedral and went into my old school shop and checked out some of the public buildings. We ended up buying a facsimile of one the gargoyles on the cathedral and it's now overlooking the kitchen door on our finca.

I can't remember the reason for this, but I'd booked us into hotel in Margate – I think it was a legacy of good times from when I was a kid. I imagine that Margate in summer remains a fun filled and interesting place, but in winter, it's right up there in the "World's most dire places" list!

Basically it was shut! Apart from one amusement arcade and a lonely fish and chip shop, there was nothing happening at all. We had a few half hearted games in the arcade and headed for the chippy, which was already starting to close. We ended up sitting in the drizzle looking at a very grey sea eating our local fare, which wasn't particularly good.

After Margate we headed to London, where we had arranged to stay with our friends Peter and Linda, who at that time had a fabulous apartment overlooking The Thames at Greenwich. We had a rip roaring time with them, having a fabulous Italian meal, then heading to an outdoor ice rink.

I'm one of those people who love to try new stuff, and I'm usually reasonably good at most things I try. But ice skating proved to be the first thing I have ever done in my life at which I was totally, completely and utterly useless! I couldn't even get around the rink, in fact I couldn't move! I staggered around until my ankles screamed at me to stop, my frustration multiplied by the fact that Julie, Josh, Lucy and all our friends were skating serenely around me and laughing their heads off. Needless to say I retired early and repaired to the nearest bar.

We saw the New Year in sitting on Peter and Linda's balcony, sipping champagne and watching the fireworks over the London eye. I knew then, that this would be our last Christmas break in UK, and the subsequent conversation with the family confirmed their total agreement. We had got to the point where England felt like a foreign country to us. Not a bad place, but not a place where wished to spend our holiday time and money. We were finally Lanzaroteños!

Chapter Eighteen - Youths United

I've introduced you to Tila and Michelle and mentioned the impact they have had on our lives already. We were sharing our office with their company Youths United, which was an organisation Tila had set up with three aims:

- To provide some spectacular sporting events
- To create and develop cultural and economic links with our near neighbours in the Moroccan Sahara
- To raise money for charities working for the Saharan people.

We became peripherally involved with YU in the year when it chose to run its first two events. The first was to be a "Quadrathlon", a race with four legs taking in three of The Canary islands. It could be done as individuals or as part of a team of up to four people. The aim was to leave the island of La Graciosa by completing a 2 KM swim to Lanzarote, climb a 600 meter mountain, then cycle the length of Lanzarote to Playa Blanca (72 KMS) and finally to sail under wind or oar power the 10KMs to Fuerteventura. Most of the entrants were doing this first event for charity and the money and stuff being raised was to be taken to Tarfaya in Morocco for The Dash, which was the second event running a couple of months later.

The quadrathlon became known as "Las Tres Islas" or the three island race and I decided early on to enter to try to raise some money for the charity L'Adaph. As a strong swimmer I had no concerns about the swim leg, and enlisted two friends, Mark to do the run and the cycle, and Ben to windsurf home. In the end our team came in third and we were very happy to have raised enough to buy a wheel chair and to have a trophy as well.

As the event date came closer, the chaos in our office gradually became unbearable, and in order to maintain our sanity, Julie and I quickly decided to help with the organisation. We spent long evenings with the team planning various parts of the event, putting signs out everywhere publicising it, and finally humouring Tila once he had a film crew from Eurosport over to cover the event. It was a complete nightmare! Tila is a wonderful person and extremely likable, but he is so difficult to work with as his attention span is very short. I seemed to slip into a kind of avuncular chairman of the board to Tila's crazy marketing director's role. The real workers in the team were Nick and Barry, who pulled the whole thing off in wonderful style.

To realise the enormity of the achievement you have to consider a number of things. Firstly we were foreigners in Spain, then we had to deal with every single town hall on three islands to get our permissions, as the event touched every district. We also had to deal with the Lanzarote government and managed to bring in both a TV crew and to get local media coverage via live radio and magazines. All this was done on a shoestring budget, funded by local businesses and run by a team of unpaid volunteers.

It is to everyone's eternal credit that the event ran, that it ran well and that everyone remained safe throughout. Las Tres Islas has run every year since, and I am enormously proud to be able to say that I have either competed in or helped to organise most year of the bizarre race, and along the way to have met some truly extraordinary people. Retired motor dealer Peter Dalkin has completed every year as a solo competitor despite approaching his 70th year. Ladies world champion kite surfer Kirsty Jones has been in it with us from the start, as have a host of minor celebrities like Scot Sullivan and Giles Vickers-Jones. But the really special people are the locals here on Lanzarote who put their heart and soul into training. I love the look on their faces as they proudly don their finishers black shirts.

Every Tres Islas finishes with the mother of all parties on the beach in Fuerteventura, and this first year we celebrated into the early hours, with poor Julie desperately sorting out the event leg times so that we could announce the winners.

A few weeks after the event, we were all prepared for the next one, which was The Dash. Tila had always dreamed of being able to windsurf from Europe to Africa, from Lanzarote to Morocco and this is what The Dash was all about. Accompanied by a flotilla of yachts, motor boats and Zodiacs, several well known local surfers and a couple of kayakers were going to try to sail across the continental divide. Julie and I joined the trip and again became involved with the organisation. After the event I wrote about it for the local newspaper, and I make no apologies

93

for inserting my story here, as it summarises the event far better than I could do so now.

The Dash 2004 – A Personal Perspective

I'm sure many other people's minds work in the same way as mine. Are the great moments you have enjoyed etched into your memory like a fantastic movie that you can replay at will, with every sight and sound captured in perfect digital format? This weekend I took part in The Dash, and there were so many great moments that I now have a whole feature film stored, and one that I will be replaying until I take my final breath. You'll be able to read the facts in many publications, and watch the film made for Eurosport television, but I would like to share some of my movie with you:

Reel One

We're aboard a Maxi racing yacht – 85 feet of taut thoroughbred racing machine. We're captained by a Norwegian, crewed by two Brits, and we have French, German, Spanish, Moroccan and British passengers – a truly eclectic and international mix, but amazingly, there are another 29 boats on the sea ahead of us, all with an international mix of people, and all with Tarfaya on the Saharan coast programmed into their GPS systems. Aboard Il Moro de Venezia, we communicate with each other in several languages, the more talented acting as translators, without even being asked. Our bond has been instant – we know this is going to be special.

Amongst the fleet there are 7 windurfers, 6 kitesurfers, a Hobie Catamaran, and a two man kayak. The last left at 3 AM, and is being oared by famous restaurant owner Kumar Dadlani, who founded the Lani's restaurant chain, together with one of his managers. It is these sailors who are the real heroes this weekend – and I'm proud to call most of them friends. Each is supported by one dedicated craft, in most cases Zodiac high speed semi inflatables. They are ahead of us because we've had some technical problems, and we're an hour and a half behind the fleet. We're on our own, but we're flat out in light winds trying to catch them. Our link is our VHF radio, and we're getting updates from the others. Amongst the crackling static, I talk to Nick and Sasha on their Hobie, to Benn on his board and

94

Benn's Dad aboard the family yacht. We're trying to be professional and maintain good radio discipline, but the excitement is in the slight choke in our voices as we realise that some of the heroes may make it all the way to Tarfaya.

At the half way stage we catch a tandem windsurfer, with their support boat close by. We run together for a mile or so, and then the boys stop for a rest and a snack. The majestic Il Moro ploughs on past, with us waving and cheering. The guys on the board look tired, but we feel we may have given them a little strength.

"Our" helicopter passes overhead at regular intervals, filming us waving and shouting. We all hope to see ourselves on Eurosport sometime soon.

We're still 20 miles out from Africa when we call ahead for berthing information and an update. We've had 7 hours at sea, and we've had to deal with some traumas of our own, but we're all elated to find out that two kitesurfers have made it! High fives and hugs all around, The Dash has been done! The Hobie's coming in too, but Benn's struggling with light winds and a hammerhead shark. Ultimately, he'll succumb to the former, unable to stay afloat – but he gets very close.

Reel Two

We're anchored off the little harbour as we're too big to go in. A fleet of little white boats have pulled up alongside, a small army of locals are aboard and we're unloading the charity stuff. We form a chain, all different ages, many nationalities, wheelchairs, crutches, clothing and kid's toys are pulled from our hold. The money to buy these things has been raised by both this event and Las Tres Islas, which took place last month. I proudly point at the wheelchair my friends and colleagues bought by sponsoring my entry into the swim leg from La Graciosa to Lanzarote. The little boats are filled one by one, and then it's our turn. We jump aboard and are motored around the harbour wall. The stink of fish is unbelievable; the contrast between our fleet and the local boats is staggering. To our left we have millions of Euros worth of yahcts, with radars and aerials and air conditioning. To our right 76 (I counted them) small wooden boats, open to the *elements and all painted green. We literally have to pull ourselves through these boats to get to some steps. As we mount them, we can see fish heads all around us, discarded from this week's catch. What looks like snowflakes blowing in the wind turns out to be fish scales – millions of them, and they are settling on our clothes and luggage.*

Their fishermen have stopped to watch us – we must look bizzare to them in our Quicksilver and Nike uniforms - all dazzling patterns contrasting with their practical and more modest garb. We are driven through the streets, Tarfaya is tatty and obviously so very poor. There is silence in our little bus as we try to take in that this place is only 100KM from our home – it shares our weather and our Ocean, but it couldn't be more different. We were proud to be bringing our charity goods, but we begin to feel inadequate, that we could perhaps have done more. There are children everywhere, but so many of them seem to be physically disabled, with club feet or damaged hands. Everyone is kept in check by armed police and The Army. They stand in neat lines watching these strange incomers.

Reel Three

What a welcome! All 220 of us have been brought to a small hotel, which has been laid out for a feast. We're all mixed up on round tables. A dreadlocked surf dude is chatting to an army officer. A Moslem lady, with only her eyes on display, is in deep conversation with a bare midriffed babe. I am talking to The Harbour Master, in a Gold encrusted uniform, and his friend from the National Guard. They are curious, and ask so many questions about our country, our lifestyle and our journey.

We form a queue for the buffet, a sumptuous feast of spicy chicken, Lamb stew, fruit and salad. There are speeches, in several languages, and the whole event is covered by local television, as well as by our crews. This has been a wonderful welcome, but we are aware that the people sharing our meal are the important people of Tarfaya, and that the real people are outside, waiting patiently to meet us.

After dinner, we walk around the town, the streets are sand, and the endless Sahara desert stretches into the distance. The houses are run down and look uncared for, the few vehicles we see are

96

rough and ready utilities – many people are travelling by donkey and cart. There are no fripperies here, nothing cosmetic, life is functional – a truck is simply a means of transporting goods or people, a house is simply somewhere to keep the weather out.

Reel Four

We are shown our encampment, which is just back from the main sandy beach. Our masts to the left, and our helicopter parked nonchalantly to the right offer yet another contrast with our home for the night. Beautiful rugs have been laid out in the centre of a three sided square of massive Bedouin tents, filled with mattresses. We have Police all around us, and a lot of the local population are here, standing at a respectful distance, but watching us and the entertainment which has been laid on. A local combo plays Arabic music at high volume. A few of our crew try to tap their feet in rhythm, and the locals sway gently to the sound.

A group of local women are painting temporary tattoos on "our" ladies feet. It sounds like the women are communicating well and finding common ground – there is much laughter.

A deal is done. We can borrow the local band's PA system. Suddenly the night air is filled with electric guitar being tuned. Galley is playing lead and about to sing, Gary is MC and has his harmonica, a cameraman pulls out an acoustic guitar, and someone is sharing the bongos with a local player. Good old rock and roll bursts forth at maximum decibels. The local crowd grows, still kept outside our camp, but they're starting to boogy now, they're clapping along with the old tunes. The women in their little circle get louder, and suddenly they're up and dancing – then there's an instant conga led by a Muslim lady with the brightest smile I have ever seen. We're all up and dancing and laughing. Victor, the bank manager and kitesurfer goes to the huge crowd and waves them into our camp – the police try to stop them, but are overwhelmed as first a few break through, and then more and more. The cops give up and stand aside, and the people of Tarfaya join us – we have finally connected, music has provided the spark and we are one big group sharing it. We sing along, we clap and we dance. Galley sings an Irish folk song, a Tarfayan sings Jimmy Hendrix. This is the moment when two

97

*cultures collided, and we all became just people – happy, smiley
people.*

Reel Five

*Early morning, and some of our guys are out off the beach on
their kites – a spectacular sight which attracts many people. The
surfers leap the waves performing tricks with the house in the
sea (built by an Englishman in the 19th century) providing an
amazing backdrop.*

*A couple of kids approach us, one has a badly withered foot,
causing him to walk sideways. They ask us in French if we have
any pens or paper. I'm distraught that we don't, and promise
myself that I will take some next year. Julie digs into her
rucksack and finds a packet of cookies. The boys look
incredulous and thank us profusely, hobbling away with their
prize hidden under a shirt. Ten minutes later, and they walk past
us with big smiles, crumbs around their faces, mouthing
"Merci."*

*It's time to head home, another long voyage. Boards are
strapped to yachts, hands are shaken all around – but we're all
thinking we haven't had enough time. Our little adventure is over
and Tarfaya begins to disappear into the haze behind us.*

*Ten miles out and the wind and sea really picks up. Il Moro heels
to 35 degrees as her great sails fill. We're making 11 knots, with
water washing over the decks. We leave the other sailing boats
behind, Il Moro coolly displaying the power that her racing
design can generate. The helicopter says hello, and the zodiacs
leap past us and we're alone again. Everyone is quiet and
movement almost impossible in the conditions. We're all given
several hours to reflect on our experiences, to have a first play of
our private movies.*

*The two Maxis arrive in Marina Rubicon together. The sun is
setting, there is a procession of carnival boats, and fireworks are
exploding. I make my final radio call with the words "Il Moro
calling all Dash vessels, we are back in port 36 hours after
departure. Thank you from all of us aboard for making this an
incredible weekend. Those of you still at sea, come home safe, we*

98

look forward to seeing you next year. This is Il Moro signing off from The Dash 2004."

As I disembark I have a strong feeling I don't want this to end. I sort of shout a general "Anyone coming for a beer in Lani's?" and instantly hear it translated into several languages. We're all tired and need to wash, so I don't expect much. We arrive at the little bar and order the first one, and something amazing happens. Small groups of Dashers arrive and add tables to ours. Within 20 minutes everyone from the big boats is there, and then people from the other boats join us. Suddenly there are ten people there, then twenty, then thirty and we're all talking excitedly about our trip. I chat with people I've never met before, and look around the table to see a huge range of ages and types of folk. We all know we have shared something amazing and we feel special and privileged. The night did eventually end, but like so much of this weekend it will stay with us all.

Epilogue

The purpose of this trip, and indeed of Youths United SL, was and is to provide an extreme sports spectacle, to help the Saharan Charity L'ADAPH, and to begin to create cultural and economic links with our African neighbours. All of those aims were achieved – although I can't help feeling we need to do more. In a time when our culture is clashing so badly with the Islamic culture generally, I feel our little band has really made some inroads in that direction, albeit with a very small group of people. I know that everyone involved, from both sides, will never forget this weekend. I feel sure we have touched the Tarfayan's life in a positive way, and I know they touched ours. The notion of a spectacular sports event, tied in with charity is an inspired one, and we all have Tila Braddock to thank for that, and of course the hundreds of people and sponsors who gave their time, money and energy to make the whole thing possible. In the cold light of day, what we achieved was small, an acorn from which a massive oak may, and should grow in the future. Imagine a world where this is commonplace, where those of us who are more fortunate can help those who aren't – not by anonymously giving cash to a charity, but by meeting the people we are helping, being part of an amazing event, and actually taking the things they need to them. The phrase "Life changing experience" is used too often, but his has been so for me, and for

99

most people involved. The good news for you is that you too, will be able share it . The planning for The Dash 2005 will begin soon – why not become part of it?

That story was well received both on and off the island and helped to publicise the fledgling organisation, which became a big part of our lives in Lanzarote. The following year I gave up a day a week of work to help direct Youths United and Julie and I were a major part of the running of the events.

YU still struggles on, but hasn't made it into the mainstream as a sports event company. But I'm sure it's only a matter of time, and even though what the team do now is tiny, it is still something hugely positive for Lanzarote and for Tarfaya.

Chapter Nineteen – Esinfo is Born!

It didn't seem to take any time at all before we outgrew the little office we shared with Youths United, and we were already looking for somewhere bigger. At this time we also needed funds to expand the website and IT side of the business and it seemed obvious to approach Tila and Michelle. They worked hard with us for a year as partners and had a positive impact on Estupendo during their time with the business, and their finance and input enabled us to take the business to another level.

Tila and Michelle had bought a derelict bar which had been on the market for some time in our commercial centre in Costa Teguise. Their original plan was to restore it and rent it out as a bar premises, and we all walked around it looking to see what needed to be done.

It gradually dawned on us that the office space at the back would be perfect for Estupendo, but the question was what to do with the huge space at the front and the sun terrace area, which had fabulous sea views.

We talked it through and came up with the vision for Esinfo. In what was to be Estupendo's home and head office for three years, Esinfo would become a meeting place, and a resource centre for people planning a move to the island, or having recently arrived. We would have comfortable couches, we'd keep the bar there to serve coffees and soft drinks, there would be a kids play area and notice boards showing items for sale and jobs available on the island.

The builders, plumbers and electricians started work at once to begin the transformation, and Julie set about buying couches, flowers and so on, while I tried to design what would become one of Lanzarote's most sophisticated internet and wireless set ups. Nick Bird, our computer guru was invaluable in this and converted my naïve design into something which actually worked, and I well remember long conversations with our electrician Mauricio about the amount of cabling needed, all the while acting as translator between him and Nick, and never repeating the swear words they were each using! "Tell him that's a f*cking stupid idea, Mike, the son of a whore doesn't know his arse from his elbow" miraculously became " Mauricio thinks

101

maybe we should rethink this one a little, Nick" and Nick's "That's because he's a totally lazy bastard, who's always looking for the easy way to do everything" would be translated as "Nick says he's happy to help do this bit, as it could be quite tricky." Kissinger would have been proud of me!

Tila and Michelle took on the bulk of the work organising the builders and the rest of us focussed on running the business. It was a pretty stressful time, but the effort was worth it when we finally opened to the public in the summer.

Esinfo was everything we dreamed it would be. A light, airy, comfortable space and a great working environment. It quickly became a beacon in Costa Tegiuse, being used by business people for meetings, locals for internet access and tourists for a coffee or a beer. Above all, it was a wonderful place to meet with our prospective clients, who could relax and not be pressurised.

Louise fell into the role of managing the front of house, leaving the rest of us to concentrate on Estupendo. We loved the way people were amazed to find an estate agent where you could have a hot shower after being on the beach, enjoy an iced coffee on the sun terrace and also buy house!

I wonder if you remember my good friend Maximo from Telefonica, from earlier chapters in this book? Well, guess who turned up to install our new telephone and internet lines in Esinfo? It was indeed the very same fellow. Amazingly he managed to get everything working successfully and without too much drama, and I had to revise my opinion of his skills.

Of course, it all went wrong three days later when first one line, then a second went down. We called it in, and Maximo turned up scratching his head. After an hour or so of running up and down the stairs he managed to get it sorted and departed again. No sooner had he left, off we went again. I had managed to sneak his mobile number, so I called him direct and got him back into the office. After a lot more digging around both upstairs and downstairs he finally came back to me and declared "It's the mice!" I thought I had misunderstood, and asked him to repeat himself "Mice are chewing the cables downstairs" He then explained to me that he would return the next day (Saturday) and put new cables in and wrap them in special mouse proof tubing and there would be no more problems. As it was now 8 o'clock on a Friday evening, I let him go and decided I'd try to sort it out on the Monday. But Maximo came good – he did come over on the Saturday morning, he fitted the mouse proof pipe, and it has worked (touch wood) perfectly ever since!

We decided to celebrate our opening by throwing a barbecue for all our customers on the island. It was a fabulous party, with more than 150 people enjoying a fabulous evening on the terrace, with some great food supplied by our butcher and cooked by our friends Alan and Tony.

We started at 5 o'clock and I expected to be finished by 9, but the party just kept going and going, and at around midnight a couple of bar owners walked in to see why this new place was the busiest bar in town! I explained that we were an estate agency, and they just laughed! I think we finally kicked the last one out at around 1 AM, and the evening was declared one of the great ones.

So Esinfo was up and running and all we had to do was focus on getting in the business to cover the huge set up costs, and once again we found that every time we expanded the business, the income grew to cover it!

During this period we decided to take on a school leaver to train up for the future, and we wrote to the various schools on the island. After interviewing many people, we eventually were stuck on two, Natalie, an English girl, and Jessica from Sweden. Being unable to decide between them, we took both on and they excelled, learning the business quickly and providing excellent support for the front line troops. Natalie eventually left us to pursue her dream career as a hairdresser, but Jessica remains with us, and we greatly benefit from her experience now and her four languages.

With Esinfo running successfully and adding incremental business to the estate agency side, Julie and I began to consider the longer term future for Estupendo, which included the idea of franchising areas of the business. This presented some problems for us, as we were having to agree strategy with Tila and Michelle as shareholders in the business. It isn't that we had problems between us, simply that it made decision making a

103

little unwieldy, and inevitably we started to think about a way of gaining complete control of Estupendo once again.

After a good deal of negotiation we all agreed on the price to buy back the 50% shares we had sold and at the beginning of 2006, Julie and I once again totally owned Estupendo, and a new phase in the company was about to begin!

Chapter Twenty – The End of Book One!

This book finished at the end of 2006, and book two is well on the way to completion, so I'll be sure to let you know when it's ready to be published as an E-Book.

I'd like to finish off with a recap on where we all were with our lives at that point:

A New Character

Louie had joined the family at that point as a rescue dog from Sara here in Lanzarote. Lucy had spent the summer working there as a volunteer, and he had arrived as a puppy, with whom she had fallen in love. It took me six long months to agree that he could come and live with us, but he turned out to be a very welcome addition to the clan, and you'll read more of his adventures in Book Two.

The Ruin

At that point we had started investing all our time and money into restoring the old ruin, which by now we were calling The Camel Sheds. Every weekend was spent labouring to keep the costs down, and Julie, Josh and I were all getting pretty fit and strong with the hard work we were putting in.

Estupendo

The business was going from strength to strength, with a settled team and some really good business coming in.

Home

We'd been lucky enough to sell our house in Punta Mujeres, but rent it back from the owners, which meant we had released the capital to carry out the restoration. We still enjoyed life in Punta, but our hearts were already in Haría and we were doing everything in our power to hurry things along so we could move "up the hill."

As 2006 drew to a close we had a chance to reflect on the fact that we were completely established in Lanzarote, and that it really was our home and our future. In the few years we had been here we had all become bi-lingual, we had established a successful business, but above all we had had great fun and many exciting adventures. The future was looking great and we were all looking forward to it!